Cast Down-God Remembers You

By:

Cherell Evans

This book is dedicated to my husband Thomas Latimer. God blessed me with you for a time such as this and I thank you for all your support and encouragement. I couldn't have done this without you and God. I love you!

Acknowledgments

I would like to thank God first. This book could not be possible if I didn't have a personal relationship with the Father. I thank you for giving me the words to place in this book and I pray that it changes someone's life and you get the Glory.

My children thank you for being understanding and leaving me in peace and quiet to meditate on the word and to write. My mom and my dad. If the last book didn't make you proud this one truly will. My husband, thank you for helping come up with the title Cast down. You're a great motivator and I get my hustle from you.
To my three teachers of the word. Thank you for feeding me the word of God. My Pastor Trvera Williams, Minister
Lakeisha Abney, and Minister Joel from my home church U-Turn for Christ Evangelistic Ministries. I honestly could not have done this without the word from you guys. Thank you for continually following in God's plan for your life. You guys truly are changing lives.

I like to thank God for staying in my life and in my heart and always being my strength and comfort when times of fear come.

Thank you to all my family and supporters! You guys are amazing and I pray nothing but blessings on your life.

Table of contents

For God has not given us the spirit of fear; but of power, and of love, and of a sound mind.(2 Timothy 1:7 KJV)

Have not I commanded thee? Be strong and of good courage; be not afraid, neither be thou dismayed: for the Lord thy God is with thee whithersoever thou goest. (Joshua 1:9 KJV)

Chapter One

The Mission

"ZACHARIAH!"

Zach was in the garden by the pond where he spent his time to praise God. It felt like only an hour that he has been there. Heaven was like a gentle massage that had you relaxed at all times. When the spirit of God spoke to you it was a calm and relaxing touch. You felt love, comfort and more joy in your spirit than usual along with just the right amount of fresh smell of flowers.

"Yes Father!"

" I AM NOT PLEASED WITH THE WAY MY CHILDREN ARE BEING TREATED ON EARTH. IT SEEMS THAT MY CHILD HAS CHOSEN THE WRONG HUSBAND AND IS IN NEED OF HELP. HE IS NOT OF ME AND HE HAS TO BE PUNISHED. ONE OF MY CHILDREN HAS BEEN PRAYING TO ME LONG ENOUGH ON HER BEHALF. SHE HAS BEEN A FAITHFUL SERVANT AND HER BLESSINGS ARE ABOUT TO COME! THE TIME HAS COME TO ANSWER HER PRAYERS AND CAST DOWN ALL HER ENEMIES. LET'S PREPARE A TABLE FOR THEM TO WATCH HER BLESSINGS RAIN DOWN ON HER."

"Yes Father, if it is your will I shall serve and protect! Who am I protecting and what is it you want me to do?"

"GO TO THE CHURCH OF CHRIST IN SIMPSONVILLE AND APPLY FOR THE ACCOUNTANT SPECIALIST POSITION. I WILL TAKE CARE OF THE REST. OBSERVE AND PRAY TO ME WHAT YOU SEE, HEAR, AND FEEL. FURTHER INSTRUCTIONS WILL COME LATER."

Zach is one of God's trusted disciples and one of many angles he sends to protect his children that believe in him. Most missions are quick and simple for Zach but this one will be a challenge and a test for everyone involved. Even Angels!

Mother Mary Stevens

Mother laid in her bed with so much on her mind. She was trying to remember and process what God was showing her in her dreams. At 65 years old with long gray hair, caramel complexion, and high cheekbones, and hazel eyes she doesn't look a day over 45. A lot of the young girls at Church of Christ pray to look like her when they reach her age. She always tells them it's because of her obedience to God that he has blessed her with good health. Mother has a spirit of discernment and a gift of dreams, these are not ordinary dreams. She can see things that will happen in the spirit realm in these dreams. When she woke up at 5am on Sunday morning she was ready for spiritual warfare. The first thing she did when she woke up and her feet hit the ground was thank God for waking her up. She put on her housecoat and her house shoes with the open toe and walked right into her closet and got on her knees.

"Lord, I come to you as humble as I know how. My children are suffering and they need your protection. Sabrina is one of your children and the sweetest woman I have come across. She is suffering and won't ask for help Lord. There are things in the spirit that you reveal to me and I know she is slowly falling into despair and depression. Someone is breaking her spirit and she is losing her faith God. Lord, I believe and receive that protection is covering her Lord. I had a dream of her crying in the corner of a room with blood all over her Lord. What Satan tries to tear her down Lord, I plead the Blood of Jesus on her Father. For I know not of your plan but I know you are great in all your ways and no weapon formed against her shall prosper. She is your child Lord. Cover her Father. I command the devil to leave her mind, right now in the name of Jesus, you have no power over her. I break every chain of depression, suicide, low-self esteem, fear, confusion, restlessness. Lord I ask you to take it away Father and cast it into the pits of hell from where it came from. Lord God give her peace Father. Show her you are by her side Lord. In Jesus name!

Lord have mercy! The devil is a liar! He has come to steal, kill and destroy. My son Jonathan! The dream of my son lying in front of the church doors bloody and bruised. Blood falling from the top of the building to the bottom, soaking into the grass, black clouds above the church. You won't win! My God is awesome and he has prepared a place for me and my child at his right hand. I bind you right now in the name of Jesus. I demand every enemy to flee, I speak life and prosperity, over his life! Joy, love, peace, and rest into his life right now in the name of Jesus!. This Church will not fall and crumble by the hands of the enemy. In Jesus precious name, I believe it is done! Amen!

Once she was finished with her prayer she got dressed, made breakfast and prepared for church. Her son Jonathan is Pastor of Church of Christ so it is her duty to make sure everything is in order and people are where they need to be. She also teaches children's church and prepares a small breakfast for the children. Just one of the ways to get the kids up and in the house of the Lord. "Lord I am ready to work and do your will, use me as you see fit" says Mother before she drives off in her 2018 white Buick Lacrosse.

Chapter 2
Sabrina's prayer

Sabrina sat in a tub of Epsom salt trying to get the aches and pains out of her body before church. She really didn't feel like going because she was really stiff. Over the past 2 years she has learned to buy it in bulk for when Max has his bad days. They have been married for 5 years and it seems to get worse every year. It's getting harder to hide her bruises. Although Max never hits her in the face she makes sure to cover that part and she buys long baggy clothes. Sabrina is 5'9" long black curly hair, brown eyes and beautiful smile. She has the shape of Gabrielle Union and long legs, D cup breast with just the right amount of butt that would make her clothes fit just right.

She doesn't wear makeup, or form fitting clothing and she never shows any skin. It's not that she doesn't have any style, it's just that Max tells her that she is his and no man should see what he has at home. He is not a Muslim but he seems to try to adopt some of their ways. To some extent she agrees but she still misses her long strapless sundresses and flip flops. She only owns one pair of open toe shoes, "It's too sexy" Max says. A gift from her friend many years ago she keeps hidden in the back of her closet. Every Sunday morning she goes through this routine. She soaks and prays to God to give her a sign, some help or anything that will reassure her that He won't be mad at her if she leaves Max. Sabrina was raised in church and she was taught that marriage is forever. The only way out is adultery or death. So she stays, prays, and soaks in Epsom salt, week after week.

Sabrina is well known in the community for the volunteer work that the Church of Christ does for the women and children at Faith Community center. She has been apart of the board for 10 years and is a mentor to many of the young girls that visit every Monday, Wednesday, and Friday. She is also one of the top realtors for Keller Williams realtors. So, she is not one of those woman that can't afford to leave. It's just…… a mental and spiritual battle that she is fighting and she feels like she is losing daily. She just can't understand what went wrong. What did she do to deserve this kind of marriage. Max and Sabrina have know each other for a total of 10 years, and he didn't show any signs of abuse until these last 2 years. They met at Church of Christ on a Tuesday night for Bible study. They were friends for 3 years, dated for 2 and married in July at Church of Christ, Pastor Jonathan provided marriage counseling and performed the ceremony. They used to attend both Tuesday and Sunday service. Max used to play the drums until he just randomly stopped going.
She got dressed in her usual church attire which is a cute blue silk blouse and a long skirt that stopped at her feet, covered in a long black thin jacket to match her shirt.

Completely covered with no makeup just lip gloss and eyeliner. She left a note for Max on the refrigerator that said his breakfast was in the microwave and that she would be back right after service. As she drove down Laurens Road she said a prayer.

"God thank you for this day that we can praise you for your wonderful ways. Protect me when I get home and heal my spirit once again so that I can be made whole. Your word is true when it says that you would never leave nor forsake me Father, but it is getting hard to smile while I am in so much pain. My mind, body, and soul is hurting Lord. I need you now more than I have ever needed you. Heal me, open my eyes so that I may see, clean my spirit so that I can rejoice with a clean heart and give me peace in and out of my home. In Jesus name Amen!"

When Sabrina walked into the Church Mother Mary was just finishing Bible study with the children and asked Sabrina to come to her office so they could pray before service. She agreed but she didn't understand why. Mother never asked her to pray with her before but the way she was feeling, more prayer is definitely needed and she welcomed it. Mother Mary was like her real mother, they have grown very close to each other over the years and there is nothing that Sabrina wouldn't do for her. Sabrina's real mother died of a cancer before she got married and her father was never in her life. She knew who he was but they didn't have a relationship because of some reason her mother never talked to her about. She just said, "Your daddy is lost in the world baby, just pray for him. He loves you, he is just lost." Her mother would say to her when she had questions as a child.

When Sabrina entered Mother's office she was waiting for her by the kneeling chair. Mother looked at her and smiled.

"Come here child we have work to do, the enemy has been busy and a war in the spirit realm is about to break out in this house," said Mother

"Yeah, he has been busy but why do you need me to help Mother? You have never asked me to pray with you before. Is this about me, if so I will be fine, I have God on my side isn't that all that I need?" asked Sabrina

"Honey, I know you are fighting demons left and right and you have been doing well on your own but God is about to send help. It will get worse before the storm clears so I need you on high alert and ready for battle. When I say this house I mean your mind, body, and spirit, including the building we are in. You are not the only one that is being attacked in what's to come, everyone will be tested. Do you trust God?" Mother asked Sabrina as serious as she could.

"Yes ma'am!" Sabrina replied.

"Do you love God and believe that he is all powerful and all knowing? And do you believe in miracles?" Mother asked.

"Yes ma'am!" Sabrina replied as tears rolled down her face.

Mother Mary had one of those spirits that when she spoke to you about yourself you just start to cry. You know you haven't done anything wrong but it's something inside of her that reaches your heart and tears start to flow. You feel love, joy, comfort, and peace all at once.

"When it gets hard and you feel like you want to give up, remember what you believe and He will work it out. Now let's get to work" she smiled.

Mother took anointing oil and placed it on her forehead as well as Sabrina's, they held hands and Mother began to pray.

"Father, we ask you come into our hearts, mind, body, and souls. You said where two or three are gathered in your name you will be in the midst of it. Although I have prayed for your child many times before we come to you in urgency Father. She is under spiritual attack and she needs your help and guidance. God, open her eyes so that she can see, open her ears so that she may hear, open her heart so that she may receive you and cover her with your blood, for Jesus died for our sins and he did not do it in vain. Protection is needed here Lord. We break every demonic chain of depression, suicide, mental confusion, heartache, low self esteem, rejection, fear, and loneliness, in Jesus mighty name. Lord you are a healer Father, I ask you to heal her heart and her body God right now in the name of Jesus. Lord we come together and put on the full body of armor as we prepare for battle for your glory. You are awesome in all your ways even when we don't deserve it or understand you. You always come through and make a way for us Lord. We are trusting you God for only you can bring us through. In Jesus name Amen!"

By the time Mother was done praying Sabrina had cried so much that her eyeliner was no longer on her eyes but all over her face.

"Mother, how did you know all that about me?" she said as she wiped the tears from her cheeks and chin.

"God has blessed me with strong discernment and dreams child. If you need me for anything just give me a call. I don't care what time it is. You are not alone in this fight honey." Mother said as Sabrina helped her off the bench.

"Yes ma'am, I will and thank you so much, I was just praying for strength and help on the way here. God is so amazing!" Sabrina smiled and laughed

"As you young kids would say Won't He DO IT!" Mother laughed and joked as they headed for the door to get ready for service to start.

When they opened the door a tall 6'4 dark skin muscular man with long dreads, bright brown eyes, full lips and pearly white teeth was standing there with his hand up like he was about to knock.

"Good morning ladies, my name is Zachariah and I was told to find Mother Mary about the accountant position available for the church." Zachariah says smiling.

Mother looked at him then at Sabrina and smiled.

"Yes, Praise God, thank you for coming. Is it okay if we do your interview after service? I am sure you would enjoy it if you stay. I am gonna need you to sit next to me though, we can't have all the single ladies not paying attention to the word now can we Zachariah?" Mother says admiring how handsome he was.

Zachariah blushed and said "Please call me Zach and I would love to stay for service it's why I came on Sunday. I know traditionally you should apply on Monday but what better day than God's day to get his work started? Trust me I am only here to do God's work." Zach said with enthusiasm.

"Where are my manners child this is Sabrina and I am Mother Mary as you have probably guessed. I see I am going to like you already, but honey you are so tall I am gonna need you to sit down when we do the interview. My neck is starting to hurt looking up at you." They all laughed and walked into the sanctuary, Zach sat next to Mother on the first row and Sabrina in her usual seat behind her.

As service started Sabrina thanked God for answering her prayers and asked for strength for what's to come in the future. As praise and worship began she noticed that Zach had a different kind of praise than others. You could tell that he loved God and was not ashamed to show it. He spoke in tongues like she had never heard it before. It had a beautiful sound almost like a violin sound. He keep his eyes closed and lifted his hands in the air. He only spoke English in some parts when he said "yes God" and "Thank you Father." When he started singing along with the praise team it was the most beautiful and relaxing sound you could have ever heard. There was so much peace and anointing on him that even Stevie Wonder could see it. Sabrina was behind him so I know Mother Mary noticed because her praise was stronger than before. As she looked around the sanctuary she noticed that everyone was either up on the feet, kneeling or looked to be praying or praising God from young to old. God was definitely present this day, once praise and worship was over they did tithes and offering and Pastor Johnathan got up to preach.

"The message for this morning is called cast down! There are many meanings and different scenarios that come to mind when you hear the word cast down but today I just want to talk about a couple. Turn your Bibles to *2 Corinthians 10:4-6 KJV For the weapons of our warfare are not carnal, but mighty through God to the pulling down of strong holds; 5 Casting down imagination, and every high thing that exalteth itself against the knowledge of God, and bringing into captivity every thought to the obedience of Christ. 6 and having in a readiness to revenge all disobedience, when your obedience is fulfilled. Now turn to JOSHUA 1: 6-9 Be strong and of a good courage: for unto this people shalt thou divide for an inheritance the land, which I sware unto their fathers to give them. 7 Only be thou strong and very courageous, that thou mayest observe to do according to all the law, which Moses my servant commanded thee: turn not from it to the right hand or to the left, that thou mayest prosper whithersoever thou goest. 8 This book of the law shall not depart out of thy mouth; but thou shalt meditate therein day and night, that thou mayest observe to do according to all that is written therein: for then thou shalt make thy way prosperous, and then thou shalt have good success. 9 Have not I commanded thee? Be strong and of a good courage; be not afraid, neither be thou dismayed: for the Lord thy God is with thee whithersoever thou goest.*

"Lord use me as you will to give the word to your children. Move me out of the way father so that I can only do your work in Jesus name Amen. Have you ever had trouble in your life and you find yourself in a battle between giving up or pressing through. The enemy attacks and we so easily want to give up and throw in the towel. Sometimes we don't even try to fight! Why is that? I have come to encourage you today! If you look in the Bible God said be strong and courageous for he is with you just and he was with Moses. There will be times when you feel like you can't take no more heartache and pain. When you even find yourself asking God why me? Where is my help? But if you look at the scripture it tells you how to get through these hard times and even the blessings that will come from staying strong and courageous. Do not look to the left or the right but only unto God for your help and guidance. Stay strong and meditate on the word day and night. Our warfare is not our battles, it's the Lord's and he will be the one to cast down all tricks of the enemy. It doesn't matter if it's your family, friends, husband or wife that is bringing the battle to you. Know how to fight in the spirit and God will handle both spiritual and natural wars for you. God told me to tell you that help is on the way! For some of you it is already here. Just open your ears, eyes and open your hearts to him and he is right there waiting with open arms to receive you. Trust in the Lord and lean not unto your own understanding because the ways of the Lord are mighty and strong. Miracles are about to happen in your life you just have to hold on and be strong." Pastor says to the congregation.

 As pastor continued to preach Sabrina started to think about her life and could do nothing but thank God and cry. She cried tears of joy for the beginning phases of starting her life over. She had come to the realization that her life was more than being in a marriage that was slowly killing her mentally, physically and spiritually. On this day things were about to change and she was going to be happy and free. No more holding her tongue when it came to Max. No more letting him control her mind and trying to save her marriage. She now knew that she was not alone and that God had her back. She could live and be happy. She just didn't know how hard it was about to be to break strongholds.

Chapter 3

War begins Now

Mother sat across from Zach after service while pastor said goodbye to the members of the church and she couldn't help but remember his praise and worship and how the glory of God truly fell in the house today. While she was praying God spoke to her and told her that Zach was an angel and was sent to do his work. So she was in awe of him and could not stop staring at him. She looked at him and said "God told me who you are and why you are here. There is no need for a interview. Bless you for coming to help us as you know we have a lot of work to do!" Mother said still staring at him

"Praise God, I am happy that he let me be known to you He also told me to tell you that your place in Heaven is set, for you have been a faithful servant of His for many years and He is very pleased with you. He hears every prayer that you have sent to him." Zach replied.

"Praise God, thank you for that message it is my pleasure to serve. It is what we are created for you know. My son does not know you are here for other reasons and I won't tell him unless God tells me to tell him. Now do you have a resume that I can provide my son with? He will want to see your credentials!" Mother stated.

Zach stood up said a prayer, God told him to hold his hand out. As he did this his hand begin to glow and a paper appeared in his hand.

Mother Mary stared at the paper in his hand with a huge smile on her face, to most people this would have them running for the door but Mother Mary was not your ordinary church goer. She and God had a personal relationship that makes her believe that all things are possible. While some people have faith the size of a mustard seed, Mother had faith the size of the world.

There is truly nothing God could not do, she was excited to see what God has in store next.

She took the paper from his hands and there was nothing on it, she looked and him and said "I don't see anything"

Zach smiled and said "That is because you know who I am, when your son touches the paper he will see all that he needs to know about my credentials and that I am very capable of performing the job that is at hand. I will be just what he was looking for. God knows what he needs and has provided it for him."

Mother shaking her head and smiling she replied "Don't you just love the Lord and all his wonderful ways!"

Zach smiles and says "Yes, but you haven't seen anything yet!"

As they laughed Pastor Jonathan knocked on the door and came in with a smile on his face and his hand outstretched for a hand shake.

"Hello, so this is the young man that has all the single women wondering who you are and where you came from. I am Pastor Jonathan Stevens it is a pleasure to meet you..."

"Zachariah, but you can call me Zach, I am here for the accountant position, Mother Mary was just interviewing me before you came in" Mother smiled and handed her son the resume.

"Oh, so it's true, no wonder I had the women asking who was with my mother, they say you have been keeping him hostage in this room." Jonathan says looking at his mother with a knowing look. She was up to something. He could feel it. *Lord please let this be the last interview, none of the five men and women I have interviewed so far have been qualified.* Jonathan thought as he released his hand and looked down and the resume.

"Now you know how some of the ladies can be sometimes, as soon as they see a new face with no ring on their finger they are going to try and make themselves be seen by any means necessary. I can guarantee you that the single and desperate will have on something form fitting and revealing come Tuesday for Bible study. These poor girls don't realize that once they stop looking for a man and start looking for God only then will the Father bless them with their husband. A true man of God does not look at your body but what your love and praise for God looks like!" Mother Mary rants while Zach just smiled and Jonathan looked from the resume to Zach, to his mother, and back to the resume. Then he stopped and stared at him.

Lord have Mercy, thank you God!", He smiled brightly "Where did you come from?" Jonathan asked looking between his mother and Zach. They both looked at each other smiled and said "From God" and they all laughed.

"Well Amen and thank you Lord, you are hired. Can you come by tomorrow at 8am? I will show you all the files and your office. Now I will warn you, it's a lot of work but I am sure you will be able to handle it." Jonathan says as he walks towards the door the go to his office.

"Oh, that's no problem sir I'll be here, Thank you very much, I won't let you down." Zach says proudly.

While Jonathan went to his office to call his wife and tell her the great news, Zack and Mother talked more about God's plan for the church.

Chapter 4

Pastor's prayer

Once Jonathan reached his office he called his wife, Tonya. As the phone rang he couldn't help but think about all the Sundays that she had missed being at church. She would always have a reason or excuse as to why she could not make it. Most of the times her excuse was that she was sick this morning as every other Sunday in the past year and a half. Two years ago he could have sworn that she was pregnant, she was gaining weight and had morning sickness. Then one day when he came home from a business trip she said that she had been sick for a few days and stayed in bed and slept all day. He begged her to go to the doctor but she said that she would be fine it was just something she ate. He also noticed that they were not as intimate as they used to be, what was once an every other day occurrence turned into once a week, then once a month. He couldn't remember when was the last time he made love to his wife. There was always an excuse. Pastor did not want to believe that his wife was cheating but she was showing all of the signs. Missing Sunday service could be overlooked sometimes if she was out doing God's work and the congregation was starting to wonder and talk. There is nothing worse than the congregation thinking badly of the First Lady. They would need to have a serious talk and real soon he thought.

"Hello Tonya, how are you baby? I have some great news! Are you feeling better I can bring you something back from the store if you need it?" Pastor says excited.

"Ummm, Hi baby, I am at the store I had to run and get something for my stomach. I am on my way home now, what's the good news?" Tonya said with hesitation in her voice.

"Oh, umm, baby we had Pepto-Bismol in the medicine cabinet at home. I thought you didn't feel well enough to get out of bed? You sound pretty good to me!" Jonathan replied back with suspicion.

"Well, about an hour after you left for church the pain eased up enough for me to throw some clothes on and go to the store, but I'll see you at the house when you get there. Bye love!" Tonya said rushing him off the phone.

Jonathan sat and stared at his phone in disbelief for what seemed like hours until Mother Mary came in and got his attention.

"Son, are you ok you seem to be thinking about something really hard." Mother said with concern.

"Oh hi mom, I'm ok just thinking about Tonya, she said she was sick again this morning but I just called her to give the good news about Zachariah and she said she was at the store and rushed me off the phone. It just doesn't make sense to me. She is not the same woman I married, it's like she doesn't want anything to do with me some days and she just doesn't care about our marriage anymore." Pastor says annoyed.

"Well, son you know I love everyone as God loves us but I do feel something is going on with that child. You all just need to talk and you need to pray about it. Ask God to reveal to you what he needs you to see, hear and do about your marriage he won't lead you astray. Now that I have given you my Godly advice I am just going to say this because it has been on my heart for the last 2 years. You should have married Sabrina!" She said with a raised eyebrow trying to read his reaction.

Shaking his head and laughing at his mother Jonathan said "Mother where did that come from? I did her marriage counselling to Max and performed the wedding. A blind man can see that she is beautiful but very married and in love with someone else. How can I be a man of God looking at another man's wife when I too am married?" Pastor replied amused.

"I am not saying to cheat or break up a marriage. Just remember her if things don't work out and you both become single is all I was trying to say. God works in mysterious ways baby." Mother Mary said smiling.

"I'll keep that in mind but for now I have to go check on my wife. I love you mama. Please, stay out of trouble and don't go bothering things that are not broken. I know how you can be mama." Pastor says playfully warning his mother

"Chile Please, I am just doing the work of the Lord." she says as she waves him off and heads out of the office on her way home.

Jonathan gathered his things and went to his car after speaking to the staff that stays to clean and lock up. While driving home he thought of what his mother said so he began to pray. "Lord, this may sound crazy but open my eyes so that I can see my marriage, open my ears so that I know that the things I hear are from you and not the work of the enemy and tell me what you need me to do. I am your child but I am human and this world can make things difficult in decisions on what we want versus what you want us to have and do. Work through me Lord and be with me. Let me speak only words of your wisdom and knowledge and accept whatever you have for me. In Jesus name Amen!"

Jonathan drove to his house with peace in his heart knowing that God is in control of his life and not him. His goal is to only follow God and lead by example. When he got home Tonya was not there yet so he decided to take a shower and relax. An hour later she came in the house with nothing in her hands but her purse and car keys. Tonya was 5'6, long black straight hair, Hershey's kiss chocolate completion, beautiful skin, thick hips and a big butt that could stop traffic. Some would think that she had work done but it was all natural. She wore makeup like it was apart of her skin. Jonathan can only remember seeing her without make up twice. She didn't need it at all her skin was flawless but she didn't think so. She had on a blue wrap around dress the clung to her hips and made all her curves available for view, with a V-shape neckline that had her double D breasts stand at attention. She definitely was feeling better Jonathan thought to himself. She looked like she was coming back from happy hour instead of a quick run to the store.

"Well, hello beautiful, you look great for a sick woman, did you leave the medicine in the car? I'll go get it for you." Jonathan said.

"No thank you I will get it later I ummm…. I took some in the car and I am feeling a lot better. Thank you for the compliment. What's the good news?" she said changing the subject a little too quickly for Jonathan's taste.

"Oh, we finally found an accountant for the church. He is the answer to my prayers! There is something about him though that I noticed during service. He is like no man I have ever meet, it's like you can feel the anointing falling off him. It's like God is with him when he is in the room. He gives this calm peaceful feeling that everything will be alright. You know what I mean?" Pastor asked Tonya.

"No, I don't know baby, he sounds weird to me but I am happy you found a new accountant. I'll have to meet him to see what you're talking about. I am going to take a shower and then cook dinner do you know what you want?"

"I would like my wife for dinner, why take a shower if you just got dressed a little over an hour ago anyway?" he says as he wraps his arms around her waist to give the back of her next a soft kiss. As he inhaled to breathe her in they both tensed up and she moved away from him.

"Honey you know the weather has me sweating a lot more than usual lately I just want to freshen up." She lies.

"Uh hum, Okay, you do that, you smell like a man anyway." He said only slightly joking. She did smell like Dolce and Gabbana Cologne.

"Whatever bighead!" She laughs nervously and walks away.

Jonathan shook his head and thought LORD THANK YOU FOR OPENING MY EYES TO SEE. He then headed to the kitchen to start dinner. Fried chicken, macaroni and cheese and some steamed broccoli was on the menu. Just as he was almost finished Tonya came into the kitchen.

"Thank you baby, I was going to do it." Tonya said.

"I know love but it seems you have had a long tiring day, I got it, go relax. I'll let you know when it's ready. We don't want you over doing it being that we don't know what causes the stomach problems just yet.' Pastor says.

"Ok love, I have to make a phone call, I'll meet you in the dining room." Tonya says and gives him a kiss and walked toward the bedroom.

Twenty minutes later he sat the table and went looking for Tonya towards the bedroom.

"I think we may need to stop seeing each other for a while, my husband is starting to notice my so called sick spells are happening too much and he wants me to go see a doctor. I also told you to stop wearing cologne when I come around. I think he smelled you on me." She whispered into the phone, not knowing that he was outside the bathroom door.

Jonathan stepped away from the door and went to the bedroom door.

"Baby, dinner is ready!" he called with a little more aggression in his voice than he tried to have.

'Oh, oh okay be right out, I was just using the restroom!" She lied as she flushed the toilet and washed her hands.

With a heavy heart he walks back to the table and sits down to eat. So much is running through his mind. His heart is broken because he truly loves his wife but adultery was always the deal breaker in his marriage. It's not something you can easily come back from. He started to think of their past, how they meet. How they never had children. His marriage was supposed to last forever. Everybody has problems in marriage and a lot of people work through adultery. For some reason Jonathan knew they were not meant to be together. He keep going back and forth in his mind question after question. *Should I ask her about it? Should I just pack up and leave? Do we work it out?* He didn't know what to do.

Tonya came and sat down and looked at the food.

"This looks great baby, I am so hungry." she says picking up the fork and starts to eat.

Jonathan just stared at her as she ate. *She didn't even bless the food!* He thought to himself. *Who is this woman?* he keep thinking. *Why didn't I notice until know! Angry* Jonathan got up from the table.

"I have to go pray right now, enjoy your dinner." he says and walks away headed for his prayer closet.

"Baby, are you ok? You don't look too good, I thought you were hungry" she yells down the hall.

"I LOST MY APPETITE" he screams back and slams the door.

Tonya continues to eat nervously. She finished and puts his plate in the microwave.

Chapter 5
Do you trust in God

Sabrina

Sabrina drove home with faith and joy in her heart. Not sure what God has in store for her but she knew that it would be a battle. Pulling up to her house she asked God to be with her as she goes throughout the rest of the day. Entering the house she goes to the kitchen and notices that the breakfast she cooked for Max has not been touched. So she goes to his man cave to check on him. He must still have a hangover from last night if he hasn't eaten yet. Upon approaching the door she hears him say.

"Why can't I wear my cologne I paid for it……. oh so you want to stop seeing me now? I see, so you have no plans on leaving him do you? I am just a play toy to you then….. don't hang up the phone!"

Sabrina ran back into the kitchen and tried to control her emotions. Yes, he beats on me and yes I want to leave him but he is still my husband and I do love him. I never thought he was cheating on me. I thought work was just stressing him out. We haven't had sex in a while but I thought it was because he was letting me heal from the fights. The fighting has become more frequent in the last year or so. *This is too much for me. What did I do? Who is she? Obviously he cares for her he doesn't want to stop seeing her. Does he hit her too? I have gained a few pounds but I am still fit and shaped in good proportions. Get it together Sabrina don't cry over him he is not worth your tears.* She tells herself.

Max walks in the kitchen with a towel around his waist not knowing that she was back from church.

"Oh, you're back, what's for dinner I didn't get a chance to eat breakfast" Max says without a care in the world.

"Hi baby, I was just looking to see what we had in the refrigerator. Anything in particular you would like? How about tramp, I MEAN TROUT, TROUT, FISH I mean." She says with a fake smile.

"Naw, how about steak and potatoes." Max suggests.

"Oh, I will need to run to the store then, we don't have that here" Sabrina says mad she has to go to the store.

"Ok, let me know when it's ready." he says and turns and walks out of the kitchen. When he turns around she notice that he has fresh scratch marks on his back. She gasps and looks around.
Max comes back in to warm up the breakfast she made him and she keep staring at his back.

"WHY ARE YOU STARING AT ME!" He yells.

"You, you have scratches on your back Max. Are you cheating on me?" She asks with her head down.

"So what if I am, what are you going to do about it? Don't question me, know your place and go get my dinner." He says as he get in her face.

" I, I just wanted" she tried to say.

Before she could finish her sentence his hand was around her throat and she was up against the kitchen counter. He stared in her eyes and said

"Look B****, What I do is none of your business. Don't make this a bad day for you. Go to the store and get my food. Don't make me repeat myself" he says angrily.

She couldn't do anything but shake her head up and down so that he understood she would do as he said. She was starting to get light headed so he let her go.

Sabrina dropped to the floor trying to caught her breath as she cried. Getting up and running to the front of the house. She snatched up her purse and car keys and left as fast as she could.

Once she was in the car she cried and prayed.

"God! I know you are with me and I know I asked you to open my eyes, but I don't know if I can handle this. I don't deserve this treatment. Help me stay strong and not doing thing that will get anyone hurt. I can't take not one more beating! I TRUST YOU LORD. PROTECT ME FROM EVIL." She cries and drives down the road.

When she got home and prepared dinner they ate in silence and Sabrina cleaned the kitchen, got in the shower and prepared for work the next morning. All kinds of thoughts ran through her head. Now that she was ready to leave how could she without him trying to kill her or stop her. Money was not an issue because they have a shared account but she also had a separate one as well. *Lord don't let me end up on an episode of Snapped.* She thought to herself as she laid down. *I am a Christian woman and I am supposed to love and pray for my enemy but that is so hard when you don't feel any love coming from the one that is supposed to love and protect you. Thank you for the protection Father for the rest of this night. Now that I see, can you help me get out Lord.* She silently prayed as she closed her eyes to rest.

"GO AND TALK TO ZACHARIAH MY CHILD." The Lord whispered to her.

Her eyes popped open and she thought to herself why him. He is just an accountant and he doesn't know me. She froze and tensed as Max came into the room.

"Move your big butt over so I can go to sleep" he said with an attitude and took off his clothes. He smelled like liquor and marijuana.

Sabrina moved as far as she could to the edge of the bed and thought to herself. Okay God, if that's what you want I'll go see Zach on my lunch break. Sabrina didn't relax until Max was snoring sleep. She closed her eyes and fell asleep as well.

The next morning Sabrina got up at 6:30 am to make breakfast for Max. She didn't have to be to work until 9am but she always made breakfast for him. Max is a construction worker so he has to be at work by 8 am. This is something she did even before the abuse started. One morning she wasn't feeling well and she didn't make his breakfast about a year and a half ago. He beat her up so bad that she had to call off work for the rest of the week. That was the first time he hit her. She had a swollen lip, a black eye and bruised ribs. Walking was an issue, even breathing. After that he never hit her in the face, he just damaged her body pretty badly. I guess he wanted to keep his demons in the closet, but needed her to be able to work to pay the bills. He hasn't missed a breakfast since then.

Once Sabrina arrived at work she thought about what God told her to do. She had the time because she only had to show two houses today before going to see Zach. She just could not understand why God wanted her to go see him. At one point she decided she was not going. She thought to herself *this is crazy, what am I going to say to him, Hi! God told me to come see you, soooo what ya got for me!* Sabrina laughed to herself.

She thought about what would happen if she didn't go. *It must be important so I guess I am going to go see a stranger* she thought.

"Hey girl, what you smiling about?" her best friend and co-worker Sherry said as she stuck her head in the door of her office.

"Oh, nothing just thinking about something crazy that was funny. How have you been? I missed you at church yesterday." Sabrina said as she stood to give her a hug.

"Oh, I'm as well as can be. You know Mother Mary called to check on me I heard church was amazing. I hate I missed it. It seems like I always miss it when the glory of God is strong in the house and it's something that I need to hear. I wasn't feeling well and my sister Tasha came over last night so I let her stay the night. You know I can't leave her in my house alone. The great thing is she said she is ready to go to rehab so I will be searching for a good one that is far away, So keep praying for her" She says with a smile.

"Praise God that is great I miss Tasha, we used to have so much fun back in the day. Well, when she is ready I know God will be waiting with open arms. I told her that she is still alive for a reason. Her testimony is going to save lives. You just watch and see." Sabrina says.

"Yes, I know it will be. I heard there is a new accountant at the church as well. I also heard he is very fine. You know I am waiting for God to send me my Boaz but it's nice to have some eye candy at the church. Brother Brown gives me the creeps just smiling at me with that Jheri curl juice on the back of his suit jacket." She says as she shivers from the thought of him.

Sabrina almost spit up her coffee laughing at Sherry. "Girl, you know you wrong for that he is old, that was the style back in the day."

"I know but when he gives me a hug I get a headache from the activator smell. Especially if it has been freshly done." Sherry said with a frown.

"Girl I can't with you this morning, you got my stomach hurting laughing at your silly self." Sabrina continues to laugh.

"I am telling you he could be one of the parents from Coming to America that got up off that couch, he was definitely the daddy!" She says more serious than she should.

"Okay, stop, I can't, That was funny, get out my office and go to work!" Sabrina says as she wipes tears from her eyes.

"So you just gonna laugh at my pain and put me out! Ok I see how you are. Are we still on for lunch today?" Sherry asked headed for the door.

"Uumm. I am sorry I have to take a rain check I have to go to the church on break." Sabrina said.

"Girl, as much as you be at church you should just pack all your bags, move in and marry Pastor Jonathan. But ok. I won't stand in the way of the Lord's work. See you later." Sherry says as she walks out the door.

Sabrina smiled at her friend and thought to herself, *it is the place I feel safest, I don't know about marrying pastor but if I could live in the church I truly would.*

Sabrina continued on with her day and soon enough lunch time was here. She got in her car and started to drive towards the church. The whole way there she was praying that he wouldn't be there so she could avoid the weirdness of having to tell Zach that God sent her to see him. Once she pulled into the parking lot she noticed Mother Mary's, Pastor and his wife Tonya's car in the back parking lot. As she walked to the door it was locked but she had a key for emergencies since she did more work in the church. I guess this is an emergency since God told her to come see him she thought to herself as she pulled the key from her purse and opened the door. Once inside she saw Pastor and his wife Tonya walking down the steps getting ready to leave to have lunch.

"Oh hi Pastor and First Lady Tonya, How are you today?" Sabrina smiles at them both.

Tonya just frowned and says nothing, impatiently waiting so they could leave.

"We are fine Sabrina, what brings you here this time of day? Is there anything I can help you with?" Pastor smiles and says.

"Uumm, no, I actually came to ummmm.." Not able to lie she told them the truth

"I was told to come see Zachariah, the new accountant today." she replied praying they didn't ask her why and who sent her.

"Uuumm hum, I bet you did", Tonya says under her breath.

Pastor must not have heard her but Sabrina heard her loud and clear. She never understood why Tonya did not care to be in her presence anymore. She did notice that it started around the time that Max stopped coming to church with her. *Oh, Lord I hope she doesn't think I want her man, Jesus, I don't even want the one I have at the moment.* Sabrina thought to herself. Pastor cut into her train of thought.

"Oh, I can show you where he is that way I can introduce Tonya to him as well. I was telling Tonya yesterday that its like he is sent from God. He has this peace about him you know?" Pastor says walking back up the stairs.

Tonya rolled her eyes and reluctantly followed Sabrina and her husband back up the stairs and down the hall to the financial office.

LORD, what is wrong with Tonya, be with me Lord this just got weirder Sabrina waited as Pastor knocked on the door and a strong deep voice replied.

"Come in it's open!" Zach said.

The hairs on the back of Sabrina's neck rose and she got goosebumps on her arms. Tonya must have felt it to because she stopped in her tracks and would not go any further. Pastor and Sabrina walked in and immediately she felt at peace and joy. Zach stood and smiled at her with those big brown eyes and it was like she couldn't pull away.

"Sorry to bother you Zach, Sabrina here was looking for you and I wanted to introduce you to my wife Tonya. We were just headed out for lunch would you like us to bring you something back? We are going to the Cheesecake Factory?" Pastor said as he looked around the room for his wife just now noticing that she was not in the room.

Zach and Sabrina both looked around the room as well.

"She was right behind me" Sabrina said looking at pastor and Zach confused.

"She must have fell behind, I do walk fast, hold on" Pastor says and he walks back to the door.
Tonya had her back pressed up against the wall and she was sweating really bad.

"Baby, I don't feel good can I meet him another day?" Tonya tried to whisper to her husband.

"Baby, why are you sweating like that? Sabrina, Zach come here!" He called for help unsure of the health of his wife.

Tonya, tried to move away but was not fast enough. Sabrina came out first followed by Zach.

"Oh Lord, Tonya are you a diabetic honey?" She asked as she tried to touch her hand to see if she was clammy.

"DON'T TOUCH ME!" Tonya yells. She turns her head and looks right into Zach's eyes for three seconds and she takes off running down the hall and out the door.

"Tonya!" Pastor yells.

"I am sorry you guys she hasn't been feeling the best lately, I have to go!" He says in a rushed statement and runs to the back door after his wife.

'Well, I thought coming here to see you was going to be weird, that was just crazy." Sabrina says as she turns and walks back into his office.

"What can I say some people just can't handle all this wonderfulness" Zach laughed to lighting the mood. "So what brings you in to see me." Zach asked looking right into Sabrina's eyes

"Ok, maybe this is a little weird but ummm.....God told me to come talk to you although I don't know why and you don't know me. But I do as God says so here I am, So, what do you got for me?" She laughs nervously, something she does to calm herself or she will just keep talking.

"Well, I am happy that you chose to tell me the truth of why you're here. I was expecting you and I knew you were coming. God has a way of talking to me as well. I know I am new here and you do not know me, but trust me I am only here to do God's will. God told me to tell you not to fear your husband and that He is here with you. He also told me to give you this" Zachariah says and he hands her a bottle of oil from his pocket. Sabrina is stuck in shock and does not reach for the oil.

Her mind was in overdrive. *How did he know I was coming? Don't fear my husband? No one knows about what I go through at home. Is this for real Lord, do you really hear me when I cry. God wants to give me something?*

Sabrina came out her trance and looked at Zach's outstretched hand. With a shaking hand she took the bottle of oil from him and looked at it. As she touched it the bottle began to glow just enough to have a soft glow as if it touched sunlight. Only Zach saw it glow brighter, she only thought it was the reflection of the sun coming through the windows.

"What is this? I have anointing oil at home already!" Sabrina said.

"Yes, I am sure you do but God told me to give this bottle to you. He says that it is special to Him just like you. He wants you to anoint yourself every morning when you get up after you pray to Him and tell Him what you need. Things will happen around you but just know that you are covered by the blood of Jesus Christ." Zach replied.

Sabrina began to cry and praise God right there in front of Zach. She fell to her knees and thanked God over and over again while speaking in tongues. Zach prayed for Sabrina and reminded her to do as she was told every morning. Sabrina thanked God and cried all the way back to work.

Chapter 6
Who are you?

Tonya

"Baby are you okay, what happened in there?" Jonathan asked his wife as he stood outside her car window.

"I don't know I just got really hot all of a sudden" she replied still trying to get as far away from the church as she could.

"You need to go to the doctor, your health has been going crazy lately, why won't you go see a doctor?" Jonathan says with frustration.

"I am fine, I don't need a doctor, let you tell it God can fix me so go pray about it will you and stop bothering me about a doctor!" she yells at him.

"Oh okay, I see you need some time alone, don't raise your voice at me when I am just trying to make sure you are okay. You are my wife or did you forget that?" he replied angrily.

"God no, how could I forget that, I am reminded everyday when I wake up! It's always church this or church that. Can you do this meeting, and you pray for this person. So yes I know exactly who I am married to thank you very much!" she replies with hate for it all.

"Oh so you have a problem with what I do, you knew what would happen when we married and you were fine with it. Now it's becoming to be a problem for you? Are you losing faith in God, in me?" he shakes his head not knowing what to do with the woman in front of him.

"You know what, I am not about to do this right now. We don't want to ruin our reputation as the perfect couple now do we. I will see you when you get home." she says with an attitude and drives away.

As soon as she turns the corner she picks up her cell phone and makes a call.

"Hello!" a male voice says in her ear. She has to breathe and remember why she called him. He has a sexy baritone voice. The kind that they used to play on the radio for midnight slow jams.

"Hey, we have a big problem, where are you?" she says in a rush.

"I'm at the gym" he replied

"Okay, I am on my way." she says and hangs up the phone.

Twenty minutes later she pulls up at the gym and Max gets in the car. She then pulls behind the gym so no one can see them together.

"I thought you said we couldn't see each other for a while, what's going on?" He says.

"How is your construction job going. Any new contracts lately?" She asked him nervously.

"No, why do you think I am at the gym instead of working? What's wrong?" He says with frustration.

"Well, I just left the church and they have a new accountant. I was going in to meet him but I couldn't get past the door. I broke out into a sweat and when he came out and looked at me I felt like I was on fire. I know it sounds crazy but there is something strange about him. I will not be able to get the money that we used to get. We have to figure out another way. I can't go around him or in that room. Its like some kind of force field or something." She says confused.

Max laughs at her and turns to look at her. "Are you serious right now. He is just a man, he made you feel all hot and bothered? Girl whatever, you are tripping. I know I better have my money come Friday." He says getting angry.

"I am not playing, if you think its a joke you go meet him yourself. I am not doing it." She yells getting mad that he laughed at her.

"Who do you think you are yelling at? Girl you better calm down before I…" he started to say but was cut off.

"Before you what?" she says glaring at him while reaching under her seat. " I am not Sabrina and you do not scare me. You think just because we have sex that I am yours and you can control me. No sir! You have the wrong one today. Don't make me come from under this seat. You would not be the first person that I killed. Try me if you want too." She says with the .45 securely in her hand. She has so much pent up anger it's like she turns into a completely different woman when she is mad and feels disrespected.

"Yeah okay Tonya" he says as he gets out of the car.

Tonya pulled off and she began to wonder how she ended up here. Marriage was beginning to weigh her down and being that the money was coming to an end so was her marriage. The money was the only reason she started seeing Jonathan in the first place. Tonya was raised with an abusive father. He would beat her mother and then he would beat Tonya. She would beg her mother to leave him but she stayed. Her mother later became addicted to pills and alcohol. It was her way of numbing the pain from the abuse. One night after her father beat both of them Tonya had had enough. So while he was sleep she slit his throat. When she woke up her mother so they could run something came over her mother and she set him on fire in the bed. I guess she wanted to get her revenge as well. Someone must have seen the flames and called the police because as soon as they walked out of the door the police was pulling up along with the fire trucks. They placed Tonya in a foster home because her mother was still high and drunk. The autopsy showed that he was murdered and they placed her mother in jail. They didn't even think that a 12 year old girl would commit murder. Her mom said for her not to worry and that she would take the blame, she did set him on fire. Her mother was sentence to 25 years but was killed in a prison fight 5 years into her sentence.

Tonya was filled with so much hate and distrust that she never fell in love with anyone. She only loved money and would do anything to get it. Before her and her best friend Tamika moved to South Carolina they lived in California. Sabrina got into some trouble with some big time drug dealer that she stole over 75,000 dollars from. She is on the run and can never go back there. Not knowing why Tonya wanted to up and move so fast Tamika came with her because she needed a new start. The plan was to lay low, get some regular jobs and just do small hits together. Her friend Tamika actually went to school for accounting and business management. So it was easy for them to run there scheme. Tamika applied for the job and then once she was hired she invited her friend Tonya to come flirt with the boss to distract him from watching the accounts, that they stole from, too closely. They always researched to see if the boss was a male or female, and if he could afford to lose a few thousand a month.

So when they went to Church of Christ that is what happened with Pastor Jonathan. Tamika was against stealing from the church at first but Tonya talked her into it. When

Pastor asked Tonya to marry him Tamika told her to say no. Tamika was against it because it was supposed to be an in and out ordeal. 6 months to a year and that's it. Tamika felt that Tonya was getting too greedy and she became convicted for her actions. You can't go to church and hear the word of God everyday and not feel bad for stealing from the Lord. So Tamika quit working for the church and moved out of state three weeks ago. Tonya had a very hard heart so her actions didn't bother her at all. Especially now that she was married to the pastor she felt it was her money anyway.

So now she is stuck with Zachariah as the new accountant and she can't even get close to him in order to figure out what her next move could be.

Zachariah

Once Tonya, Sabrina, and Pastor Jonathan left the church Zachariah stayed back in the office to get some work done. He didn't have to do as much as Pastor thought that needed to be done. Whoever was the accountant at first did a good job at having it all organized and readable. It looks like over the course of three years someone has been putting money into an account that is supposed to go to a non profit organization for abused women and children called A.C.E. Legaci Foundation LLC. The shelter under that LLC is called God's Helping Hands. The withdrawals and reason for them don't make sense and they are too frequent. Zachariah would give them a call to see when the last donation was given real soon.

So it was obvious that someone was stealing money. He just had to find out who and he had a good feeling on who that person was.

Zachariah felt a strong breeze across his face that felt like a light kiss on the check and the smell of fresh flower. He fell to his knees to pray.

"ZACHARIAH, TELL ME WHAT DID YOU SEE?" the Lord asked.

"Father, there is so much hatred and love in this church. It's hard to explain. The hate and cold hearted run from me and the pure at heart run to me." he replied.

"THIS IS BECAUSE I HAVE SET IT SO YOU CAN IDENTIFY THE EVIL AND GOOD IN PEOPLE. THE EVIL CAN'T STAND TO BE IN THE LIGHT AND EXPOSED FOR WHO THEY ARE." God says.

"Father, I gave Sabrina the oil and told her to anoint herself everyday. May I ask what is in the oil it glowed when she touched it." he asked the Father.

"THE OIL IS A COLLECTION OF HER TEARS AND HER PRAYERS, SHE GAVE THEM TO ME SO I HAVE GIVEN THEM BACK AS AN ARMOR OF PROTECTION FOR HER" God says.

"What do you wish me to do about Pastor Jonathan? His wife is full of evilness."

"RIGHT NOW JUST BE A FRIEND TO HIM, TALK WITH HIM. WHEN THE TIME COMES HE WILL NEED HELP ON HOW TO HANDLE ALL THAT WILL BE REVEALED TO HIM AND WHAT TO DO WITH IT. RIGHT NOW HE IS STILL PRAYING TO ME FOR GUIDANCE. WHEN HE STOPS PRAYING TO ME AND IS FILLING UP WITH TOO MUCH EVILNESS GO TO HIM IMMEDIATELY" God replied.

"Yes father." Zach replied.

"I AM PLEASED WITH HOW THINGS ARE GOING SO FAR. MY CHILDREN ARE STAYING STRONG AT THE MOMENT BUT THERE WILL BE A TIME WHEN THEY WILL START TO LOSE FAITH IN ME. TIMES WILL GET HARDER BEFORE THEY CAN UNDERSTAND THAT THERE IS ALWAYS A PURPOSE IN THE WAY I DO THINGS. THIS WILL MAKE THEM STRONGER AND THEIR FAITH WILL NEVER WAIVER AFTER THIS STORM." God says.

"Yes Father. I understand." Zach replied

"ZACHARIAH, I MUST WARN YOU, THIS WILL BE CHALLENGING FOR YOU AS WELL. THEY WILL TRY TO CRUCIFY YOU. REMEMBER WHO YOU ARE AND WHY YOU ARE HERE. God informed Zachariah.

"Yes, Father I KNOW." Zach says in a whisper and the presence of the Lord left him.

Mother Mary was on her way to her office when she felt a breeze and the smell of fresh flowers. She looked around and noticed that a bright light was coming from Zach's office.

"ALL WILL BE WELL SOON MY CHILD" God's voice whispers to her.

"I know Lord, I know" she says and smiles then walks to her office to get ready to leave for the day.

Max

Max walked back in the gym trying to figure out what his next move would be. He couldn't continue to go to the gym so he had to actually find a job in construction. He first met Tonya at church. At first he was ignoring her advances but the flesh is weak and what was supposed to be a friendship turned into something more. A lot more than what he could bargain for. Everyday he learned something new about Tonya and he was starting not to like who he saw. She played like this sweet innocent woman of God but she was truly a killer and a gold digger. Max had control over Sabrina but he could not control Tonya the same way. That was one of the things that Max liked about her. Tonya was not weak and did not care about love in any way possible. She trusted no one, not even her perfect pastor husband. This made it easy for their situation for him. No strings attached and he didn't have to worry about Tonya telling his wife of his infidelities, she knew her place and played it well.

When Max meet Sabrina she was a breath of fresh air. Sweet, caring, helpful, faithful and would do anything for him. That was back when he was in a bad place and had nowhere else to turn but to God to help him get through his hard times. He couldn't find a job, his mother had died from the hands of his abusive father and Max begged her to leave. Even as a child he would cry and beg but she didn't believe in divorce and she refused to leave or tell on her husband to the police. So as soon as Max was of age to move out he did just that. His father never beat him but he was verbally abusive. He would say thing like "Max will never be anything in life but another statistic. Another black man that would end up dead or in jail like the rest of his friends."
When he walked in the church Pastor was there and so he asked if he could help him find work while he stayed in a shelter. Pastor asked what kind of skills he had and learned that Max could play the drums and was good with his hands so he hired him to be the drummer and help with the things around the church that needed fixing. Eventually, he found a job with a construction company that Pastor referred him too. Things started to look up for him so he followed God's word and eventually found a wife. He thought he was ready until temptation came knocking on his door. Max felt so bad for his betrayal that he stopped going to church. He couldn't look at the man that had helped him so much and continue to sleep with his wife while also living off the money that they stole.

Max was angry with himself and all the hurt from his mother passing and his father's abuse that he took all his frustration out on Sabrina, At times he wanted to ask God for forgiveness but he felt he was not worthy of his love and grace so he submitted to his evil ways and stayed that way. Max felt he was beyond forgiveness especially from Pastor Jonathan. He is a good man but even this was far more than betrayal. He felt no man could forgive him for that. God maybe, but not man. No way!

His anger became uncontrollable when he had gotten Tonya pregnant about a year and a half ago and she refused to keep the baby. Max had always wanted kids to prove to his father that he could be a better man than him but she refused. She didn't want kids and Sabrina had not gotten pregnant yet. This was when he thought he was actually in love with Tonya so he wanted to move away and they could start over. Tonya laughed in his face and said he was stupid to think that she would leave her financial security for someone that could not do half of what Pastor provided for her financially. That was the first morning that he beat Sabrina. It was over something so simple and stupid. He didn't have his breakfast like he did every morning so to see that she wouldn't do something so normal and show that she cared it broke something in him and so he resorted to becoming like his father. Angry and mad at the world for his shortcomings in life. She was just like his mother, she never called the police or tried to leave him. Now he sees why his mother never left. The only difference was Sabrina actually had the money and support to leave if she chose to so he felt she really did love him. He instilled fear in her every chance he could. All he had to do was raise his voice at her. She was too scared to leave him. He actually did need and love her. He would be on his own again if she left him.

Max finished his work out and put his work clothes back on. There was no need to take a shower because he had to make Sabrina believe that he was hard at work.
Once he made it home he took a shower and tried to think of a way to tell Sabrina that money will be slow on his end for a while. He would just tell her he finished his assignment and had to look for more work. It's not like it hasn't happened before. She is afraid of him so she would not question him. No problem at all he thought.
Sabrina came home an hour and a half after he did at about 5:30 p.m. He noticed that she looked like she had been crying but she seemed to be happy. Well he wasn't happy so he was about to ruin that good mood of hers.
"Hi baby, how was work?" she asked with smile on her face and she gave him a kiss on the cheek. He looked at her like she was crazy, she hasn't done that in a long time. *Is she cheating on me or something* he thought.

"It was straight I finished my work assignment so money will be slow on my end for a while until I find another one." he said with that attitude.

"Oh okay, no problem, you know I can handle the bills until you find work." she says blowing it off like it was nothing.

He stared at her and noticed that she had a glow to her that hadn't been there before. *Who is making her so happy all of a sudden.* he thought to himself. *It has to be another man.* He thinks to himself.

"I didn't need the extra information Sabrina. All you need to say is okay and no problem. What you think I can't find work or something? Like I'm just going to live off you? You think I need you is that what you're trying to say?" he said getting angry for no reason.

Sabrina stopped in her tracks on the way to the kitchen to start dinner and looked back at him confused.
"No Max, I know you're not that kind of a man. I was just letting you know that I got your back. We are a team when one falls the other picks them back up that's all baby." she says nervously waiting for his next response.

"So you think I've fallen off my game now is that what you're trying to say?" he says getting closer to her like he's about to strike her but he suddenly stops. He couldn't even talk anymore his breathing became labored and he begin to sweat and cough really hard. She ran to the kitchen to get him some water he noticed that as she moved away from him his breathing became normal but he continued to sweat. As she got closer he couldn't breathe again so he waved his hand for her to move away from him then he begin to breathe normally again.
What the hell was that he thought. He no longer had mean and evil thoughts of things to do to her as his mind tried to figure out what just happened.
"Are you okay baby do you need anything?" This time as she got closer nothing happened. He was no longer mad at her so he could breathe properly to give him the water and he drank it.

"Thank you, I am fine. I am going to take a nap be quiet and don't bother me" he said frustrated because he couldn't figure out what just happened.
Maybe it wasn't her it was just something in the air. Yeah that's it! I am just tripping man I've got to stop smoking weed. I am acting like Tonya and that account! he thinks as he gets in the bed for his nap.

Sabrina just stood in the hallway for a while trying to figure out what just happened with Max. *It was like he couldn't even get mad at me.* She thought to herself. She had put the oil on before she came in the house. She was in a great mood from the meeting with Zach of course. She had no clue on how the oil would work and she wasn't trying to find out either. Overjoyed with the way the oil worked for her she put her Bluetooth in her ear and turned on her Tasha Cobbs iHeartRadio to give God his praise while she cooked dinner. She tried to keep her singing down so she didn't wake Max up. *God is just too good to me. I have to praise Him the right way.* She thought and so, she sung with her whole heart "*For Your Glory I would do anything just to see you, to behold you as my king*" as she sung song after song tears begin to form and pour down her face. She had to stop and get on her knees and praise God as Break Every Chain begin to play by Tasha Cobbs. She felt her chains being broken at that very moment.

Unnoticed Zachariah stood in the kitchen watching her with approval for the praise she was blessing the Lord with. Zachariah joined in and praised God with her and her praise went into overdrive. The holy spirit fell on her right there in the kitchen and she began to speak in the tongues. He watched her until she laid down to close her eyes.

 Zachariah went to find Max in his man cave playing the video games and smoking marijuana. He watched him and listened to his thoughts. He was thinking of another woman lustfully. When he had thoughts of going to wake Sabrina up for a little fun he began to sweat and lose his breath. The thought he had of Sabrina were not of love making but of torture. As he coughed and tried to catch his breath he looked around. He could feel someone in the room with him but he just couldn't see them. Zachariah continue to watch Max and eventually he looked into his eyes. He was able to see his soul and heart. There was no love in his heart just hatred and anger. Max stayed in the same spot for 2 minutes in a trance as he continued to sweat like he was in a sauna.

Disappointed in what he saw Zachariah released him from the trance when he looked away. Max continue to cough uncontrollably. Zachariah left the house for he had no worries for Sabrina that night as she slept.

Max finally got his breathing under control and when he got his mind to cooperate he was really, really sweaty so he decided to take a shower and go to bed. He didn't know what was going on but he was definitely going to figure it out.

Chapter 9
The Truth hurts

Pastor was in his prayer closet trying to figure out what was going on with his wife. *She used to be so sweet, faithful, caring and obedient. Not just to him, but to God as well. Was it all just an act? Who can act for four whole years? Was I so blind with God's work that I missed the signs? Did I change? No, my schedule has stayed the same. Maybe a few out of town trips but nothing over a three days stay. I have tried to give her the attention she needs. We even have our dates every week and vacation twice a year for a whole week at a time. I give her the space she needs so she can have that alone time as well as girls trips with her friends. Do I try to save my marriage or let the chips fall as they should.*

After thinking hard and coming up with nothing he gets on his knees and prays to God.

"Father! What do I do about this? I thought I had a good wife for me. I still love her Lord, I want us to work but I can't stay married to someone that is not of you. It's like she doesn't believe in you. If she doesn't believe in you how can she believe in me Lord. She is cheating on me God! I can feel it. She is a wolf in sheep's clothing and she has come to steal, kill and destroy the work I have put in for you Lord. What am I to tell the congregation? This is not just about me but about the many souls that could get lost in this situation. Lord, I pray that whatever you have me do that it does not turn the people away from you in Jesus name Amen."

Pastor was in his closet so long that he didn't hear Tonya come in and cook dinner. She knew he was in there and she knows not to bother him while he is in there as well. It was his peaceful place and his alone time with the Lord. He walked into the kitchen to see her eating and she didn't even look up to greet him. So he made his plate and sat down. After he prayed over his food and ate his fill she still had not said anything. She was done with her food and got up to put her plate up.

"Hey, can we talk? You haven't said a thing to me or even looked at me during dinner." Pastor says as he gets up and follows her into the kitchen with his own empty plate.

"No I'm not in the mood to talk right now." she replied with attitude.

"Well don't talk just listen. I have been praying and .." Pastor started but was cut off by Tonya.

"God! Does it always have to be about God and church? I don't want to hear it!" she yells at him.

Shocked from her reaction Pastor just stares at her like she had horns coming from her head or something.

"First stop yelling, second, no it's not always about God. I want to know what is going on with you. Are you cheating on me?" He asked with a knowing look.

"You know what, I am not doing this" she say as she walks toward the bedroom. Pastor follows her and she rolls her eyes. She is more frustrated that he won't leave her alone.

"It's a simple question. Yes or No? You seem to be very vocal on what you're not going to do so let's talk about what you have been doing lately. I notice you miss church a lot more. You claim to be sick and in bed before I leave but when I get back you are either not here, fresh out the shower and you always have your makeup done. You only do that if you are leaving the house. Not only that I could have sworn you were pregnant a while back. To make matters worse we haven't had sex in a very long time now or in that time frame I believe that you were pregnant. So you want to tell me what you are doing instead of what you are not going to do. I am not stupid Tonya." Pastor says trying not to raise his voice.

"You know what, fine! I have been cheating on you! With who is none of your damn business. Now you want to talk, let me tell you what you are not going to do. You are not going question me and you are not going to divorce me either. I will make your life a living hell. I know how much that church means to you, I will burn it to the ground first. There is so much you don't know about me my dear sweet husband. I am not the woman you think I am. I am capable of many things." She says in a calm angry voice.

"So if you're cheating. You obviously don't love me or want me so why stay?" Pastor asked sad, mad and hurt. He was looking at the woman he married and she was gone. It was like watching a crazy person with multiple personalities switch from person to person.

Tonya smiles like someone just offered her a million dollars. "Baby, you love me that's sweet. I don't know what love is but if you must know, for the money, security and a occasional good lay. Why else stay with someone?" she replies without a care in the world.

"Wow!" Pastor was beyond angry. He truly did not know his wife. The things he wanted to say and do would not be pleasing in God's eyes so he just walked out the room. He went to get his keys and drove off into the night.

As he drove down the street his mind began to race. *What does she mean I don't know her and she could make my life hell?* He decided to go to the church. He was going to sleep in his office tonight. The thought of laying next to Tonya made him sick to his stomach. He went right into the church and fell to his knees at the pulpit.

"Father this is becoming to be a bit much. I know I wanted the truth but this is more than I bargained for. When I took a wife it was for better or for worse. Well, this is the worst. How can I overcome this when I truly love my wife. I feel I need to leave. You are against adultery. I forgive her but it's hard to really forgive someone when they show no remorse for hurting you and keep doing it. How am I supposed to trust her after this Lord? She is a liar and now I see she is nowhere near the woman of God I thought she was. How could I be so stupid and blind not to see her for who she really is Father. Please help me! I need you right now, what do you want me to do?"
"JONATHAN!" God whispered in his ear

"REMEMBER YOU ARE MY CHILD. DO NOT FAINT FOR THE BATTLE HAS JUST BEGUN" God says.

"Yes Lord, I remember but what am I to do?" Pastor replied.

"GO SEE ZACHARIAH" God says.

"What, but why Lord?" Pastor asked confused.

"DO YOU NOT TRUST ME CHILD, WHY QUESTION ME?" The Lord said.

"I am sorry Lord, yes I trust you" Pastor replied.

"THEN GO SEE ZACHARIAH TOMORROW, BUT FOR NOW I GRANT YOU PEACE AND MUCH REST. YOU WILL NEED IT" God say and leaves Pastor's presence.

"Yes Lord. Thank you Father!" Pastor replied

Pastor went to his office and pulled out his fold out bed from the couch. He laughed to himself thinking. *I thought mother was crazy when she begged me to buy this thing. I am glad I listened. I thought I would never need this thing. Thank God for mothers.* He got sheets and covers from his closet and rest in peace with no worries.

Zachariah watched Pastor fall into a deep sleep and God called out to him.

"ZACHARIAH" God said.

"Yes Lord?" Zach replied

"IT IS TIME FOR HIM TO SEE THAT SHE IS MANY! HE WILL ASK FOR HELP AND I WANT YOU TO SHOW HIM EVERYTHING. IT IS TIME FOR THEM TO BE CAST DOWN INTO THE PITS OF HELL FROM WHERE THEY COME." God says with authority in his voice

"Yes Lord it will be done." Zach replied

Chapter 10
God's Grace

Sabrina

The next morning Sabrina got up, anointed herself with the oil and prayed. She got in the shower, made breakfast and left for work. She was feeling great as she hummed and sang, *"Our God is greater, awesome in power, Lord you are higher than any other!"* She couldn't remember all the words so she sang what was in her heart that morning. She didn't even get to sit down good before her best friend Sherry came in and sat in the chair across from her desk.

"Good morning Sherry! How are you this morning?" Sabrina asked smiling from ear to ear.

"No my good friend, the question is how are you?" she asked as if she knew something Sabrina didn't.

"I am great! Why are you looking at me like that? Sabrina asked confused.

"Well, the last time you have ever walked in this office singing and smiling was when you first meet Max. So, either you are cheating, you guys reconnected or Jesus is coming back to have lunch with you today instead of me!" Sherry jokes.

Sabrina just laughed and shook her head at her friend.

"Girl you ain't got the good sense God gave you. I just know that God is good. Is that not enough for me to smile and be happy about?" Sabrina asked knowing her friend was about to say something else crazy.

"Ummm huh. I noticed that since you went to church on lunch you have been awfully chipper. So is it Pastor Jonathan that has caught your eye or the new accountant Zech, or Zach whatever his name is. I heard he was heaven sent you know." Sherry says smiling.

"Girl his name is Zachariah and neither him nor Pastor has caught my eye. Just the Lord above. I am a married woman and you know I take my vows seriously." *Seems I am the only one that does.* She thought to herself placing a smile on her face.

"Maybe I need to attend service tonight and get a good look at this Zeck guy. I want to be singing and smiling like I just had a great night with a man that took me to heaven and back too!" Sherry says.

"Oh my goodness, girl, there is nothing of that nature going on over here. God is just good. I do think you should attend church tonight. You know you need Jesus right?" Sabrina laughs at her joke.

"I'll have you know that me and Jesus got a special thang going on!" Sherry says folding her arms above her chest.

"Yeah, you do, kind of like a complicated relationship on Facebook, on again, off again" Sabrina laughs.

Sherry just smiles at her friend, happy that the old Sabrina is coming back out to play. The one full of love, joy and fun. The strong woman of God she met when she started working for Keller Williams Realtor. If it wasn't for Sabrina Sherry wouldn't know God at all. She would still be out sleeping with every man that showed her some attention and in the club partying. Sherry was a beautiful woman but she lacked self esteem. She was the tomboy growing up and she looked like Lupita Nyongo from Black Panther with her short hair, dark skin and beautiful smile and fun spirit. She was always the life of the party. She just can't seem to find a husband.

"Yeah, ok, that's a good one and I am loving this side of you so I am gonna let you have that one. I will see you at lunch." Sherry says and goes back to her office.

As the day went on Sabrina was on cloud 9 all day, she closed two houses this morning that cost over half a million dollars. And all that was needed to do was to finish her paperwork this afternoon.
Lunch with Sherry was fun as usual. For a long time lunch with Sherry was always the best part of her day. Sabrina looked forward to it when she wasn't in her right state of mind. Sherry has this way of lifting her spirits without trying. Mother Mary called to check on her as she does two to three times a week and made sure she would be at church tonight.

When Sabrina got home she cooked a quick dinner while Max was in his man cave drinking and smoking weed. She was going to ask him to go to church but not in the state that he was currently in. She also didn't want to start a fight like last time. She almost didn't make it to church that night. Her body was so sore after that beating. Sabrina never could get with smoking. She didn't like not having control of her thoughts.

She only had a glass of wine for special occasions and never had more that two. She could never over indulge like her friend Sherry. Even Sherry had cut back on drinking. She learned her lesson when she went out with some people she thought were her friends and had too many drinks. She was raped by the taxi driver. Her friends left her in the club so she had to call a taxi. She sued the company and they guy was put in jail. Let's just say the amount of money she was awarded, she doesn't have to work if she doesn't want to. She does it for something to do. This was when she was introduced to God by Sabrina. She couldn't handle the shame she felt even if she was the victim and won the case. She gave ten percent of her award to the Church of Christ.

As Sabrina got dressed for church she thought of what to wear. She was feeling good just a little stiff. Plus her bruises had not healed yet. She took out a long black dress with long sleeves and a red belt to go with her necklace and earrings. Thinking about her friend she smiled and went into her closet and pulled down the Christian Louboutin Black open toe red bottoms Sherry bought her as a gift for introducing her to Jesus that she never got to wear.

"Perfect" she said out loud. *Lord cover me as I attempt to wear these shoes.* She prayed to herself. She has had these shoes for three years and never got a chance to wear them. Now was the best time to try them out. It's sad when you can't wear your favorite shoes because your husband thinks they are too sexy. "No man should see you in anything sexy except me, that includes shoes" she remembered him yelling after he had punched her in the stomach for having shoes on that only showed her first two toes and a strap around the ankle.

She stepped in Max's man cave and said "Honey I am on my way to church. Dinner is on the stove. I will clean up when I get back." Hiding her feet behind the couch she leaned over the back of the couch to give him a kiss on the forehead.

"Okay, bye" he said.

She was almost out of the door.

"Sabrina, nice shoes, you look great! Are those new?" He says holding back his attitude.

She stopped nervously and looked down at her feet. Praying in her head. *Please God cover me!*

"Oh these no, Sherry bought these for me years ago. I just never got a chance to wear them." She replied putting on a fake smile

"Sherry huh? The loud mouth friend from work? They look expensive. Are those red bottoms?" He asked only knowing what they are because Tonya has a lot of them.

"Yes, she is a good friend, I would hate for them to go to waste in my closet. I figured I could wear them at least once you know. She did pay a nice amount of money for them." She pleaded with him.

Max began to get mad because she knew he did not allow her to wear shoes of that fashion. He could not open his mouth to say anything because he started to sweat. He just nodded his head and waved her off.

Sabrina left the house all smiles for this small win. She could finally wear the shoes. She prayed Sherry was at church tonight so she could finally see her in them. When she parked her car in the parking lot she saw Sherry getting out of her car. She hurriedly walked over while she was reaching for her Bible. Sherry looked Sabrina up and down and smiled so big you would have thought someone offered her a million bucks.

"Yesssss, you are wearing the shoes and you look great in them. Give me my props, I got taste right? I thought you didn't like them because I never seen you in them." Sherry says giving Sabrina a hug.

"Oh no I love them, they are my favorite shoes I just couldn't wear them" she says lowering her voice so no one would hear her.

"Oh, honey, did he see you leave with them on?" She asked Sabrina scared that she might have risked her life just to wear a gift she bought her unknowing what kind of man Max was.

"Yes but as you can see God is working. Let's get in here and thank Him properly shall we!" They laughed and high fived each other.

"You don't have to tell me twice" Sherry replies happy that her friend is breaking out of this stronghold.

Sherry knew that Max was abusive to Sabrina but she never intervened. She knew that when her friend was ready she would tell her. What Sabrina didn't know was that the ten percent that was donated to the church she asked Pastor if he would be willing to open a shelter for women and children in need of help with abusive spouses, rape victims as well as runaway teens. Sherry works at God's Helping Hands in her free time mostly on weekends when she knows that things get crazy around that time. Sherry even teaches a victim awareness class. Sherry knew the signs of when a woman was at her breaking point of leaving. Sabrina was showing those signs. Sherry learned the hard way not to intervene when an old friend of hers was in an abusive marriage. She tried to help her escape with the kids one night and the husband returned home. Her friend made her leave without them and tried to play it off like everything would be ok. Sherry even sent the police to her house to check on her that night. She was too late. Because when he saw the bags packed he flipped out and killed her friend and the two kids including himself. It broke her heart but she promised she would always help but in different ways.

Once they were seated and waiting for service to start. Mother Mary and Zachariah came in and sat in front of them.

"Oh, my Lord, Is that Zech" Sherry asked Sabrina in a whisper staring at Zach from behind.

Sabrina laughed at her friend and said "Yes, That's ZACH-ARIAH. Remember you are in the house of the Lord now keep your thought on God and not Zachariah" Sabrina said as she stood up to pray.

"Guuurl!, Okay, Lord be with me he is definitely heaven sent" Sherry said standing next to Sabrina.

"Stop it Sherry!" Sabrina said fussing at her friend like a kid in a candy store.

Unknowingly, Zachariah heard all that Sherry had to say about him. He just smiled to himself because he knew she was a woman of God she just liked to have fun. After prayer, the praise team sang their version of Ordinary Worship by Kelontae Gavin. The girls noticed that as Zach prayed while the intercessor prayed it was like he was feeding the words to her or something. His lips almost matched hers. Prayer was everything they needed to hear. By the time Pastor Jonathan took to the pulpit they were starving for the word.

"Good evening! I know you all came here for the word but I will not be preaching tonight." The congregation looked around in confusion some looked at Mother Mary. She would preach when Pastor was not there sometimes.

"The Lord told me to give the pulpit to a certain woman of God today. She has a word for you all. Now she does not know about this so I pray that you will be welcoming to her voice. I also pray she won't be to upset with me for putting her on the spot. I am only doing what the Lord says. Sister Sabrina, can you come up here please?"

Sabrina was shocked he said her name. She went to looking around for someone else named Sabrina then looked at Pastor when no one else stood up. "Me" She mouthed to him and pointed at herself.

"Yes you! No other Sabrina in this church but you. God showed me your face to verify it was you. He says you have a word for us and a praise you need to release to him." Pastor replies to reassure her.

She looked at Mother Mary, Sherry the congregation then at Zachariah. When she looked at him she heard the word FEAR and stood up. The congregation began to clap and give her words of encouragement. Cheers and love filled her up. Her silly friend Sherry even did the Arsenio Hall cheer with her fist in the air. She laughed at her and made it to the pulpit.

"I know this may seem crazy and you technically are not a pastor but God can give a homeless person a word to give to the rich. Trust in God and let him use you." Pastor said as he helped her to the podium.

Mother Mary just smiled and looked at them interact. *They have no idea what God is doing. They look so beautiful together up there and they don't even see it.* She looks at Zach and winks her left eye.

Surprisingly, Sabrina was not uncomfortable at all. It felt right to her. Peaceful even. She looked at Pastor smiling at her as he sat in his chair beside her. Mother Mary, Sherry, and Zach all giving smiles of encouragement. *Lord, I am here, use me as you will.* She silently prayed.

"Well, when God say go and do we must do it huh." She says laughing "Can't say no to God can you?" The congregation agrees with amens. Well, Thank you Pastor for listening to God and I know he will bless you for it. God works in mysterious ways doesn't he? As I was getting up and looking around the word FEAR came to me. Look at 2 Timothy 1:7 for me. *For God Hath not given us the spirit of fear but of power, and love, and of sound mind.* It's so amazing and funny that he would give this word to me when I am one to struggle with fear myself. You all know I don't talk much. I am a servant of God and I go home. My closest friends know most of my fears. *Serve and go home.* Serve and go home. That is what I did. No one knew I was fearful of people because I did serve and go home. I was fearful of what they thought about me, what they would say. I was fearful of hurting someone's feelings. Fearful of not helping someone that really needed it. Fearful of my true life at home....." She paused and looked at Mother Mary and Sherry as tears formed and ran down her face. "I was fearful of dressing a certain way. Scared to walk out of my house with these very shoes on.... Have you noticed that my body is forever covered up. I don't wear tight clothing or show any skin. It's not that I am one of those overly religious woman that believes you can't wear certain things to church. This is not that kind of church, thank the Lord for that. It's also not that I don't like style. I actually love a little skin here and there showing.. It's because I was fearful of what you would say if you saw my bruises.... Not just the one on the surface but the ones that are deeply wounded in my heart. The spirit of fear can put you in a cage. Lock you away for no one to see. A spirit of sound mind, power and love. You know the spirit of fear can turn your mind into a cage and you won't have the keys of power and love to set you free. But if you call on Jesus! The one that rose from the grave with all power in his hands!...... *And I will give unto thee the keys of the kingdom of heaven: and whatsoever thou shalt bind on earth shall be bound in heaven and whatsoever thou shalt loose on earth be loose in heaven Matthew 16:19* pray to God to loosen those chains of fear, so that you can break free from that cage. Bind the spirit of depression, low self esteem, laziness, adultery, lust, and suicide. Ask for your help and you will get it! Too many times we miss out on our blessing because fear holds us back. God calls you to minister to your neighbor but you're too scared of what that person might say about you.. So you say no to God and you miss out on him trying to bless you. That person you said no to not speaking what God told you to tell them, had the keys to your new job or the money you needed for that bill. That spirit of laziness, procrastination, unworthiness will really have you in a cage. You won't apply for the job because you feel you are not qualified. Or you wait too late to apply and the position is taken, just being lazy. I'll do it tomorrow. God says do it now. The time is now, your blessing is now! If you step away from fear and ask for help.

The Pastor, Zach, Mother Mary, Sherry and the whole congregation were on their feet, shouting Amens!, Preach Sister! Some were even crying.

"Don't be afraid of what the world thinks of your life! God holds the keys to our peace of mind, our joy and our love. He knows who is right for us. We as humans get so caught up in; I just need a husband/wife so we can stop sinning that we don't stop to take the time and ask God to show us their spirit, their prayer life. God is this man or woman from you Lord? It's hard not to lust over someone you have been dating for a while. So you hurry up and get married."

"You better preach that daughter" Mother Mary yells waving her tissue.

"I know, I have been there. Then you are fearful in your own house. They know too much about you now. They know how to keep you caged in fear now. Scared of saying or doing the wrong thing. You don't want people to know because you're ashamed or scared of what they might do or say. That spirit of fear has you again. Bondage, Soul ties!! But God! When I tell you that prayer and fasting works. God works! I am a living testimony. It's funny that God will have you minister to others while you're in your own storm...

Sabrina began to sing from her heart to God at that moment. *I'm calling you Jesus! I'm calling your name! I'm saying I love you! I need you today! I need you forever and I'm praising your name! I'm Calling you Jesus! I'm calling your name! I just want to say that you Lord! You open my eyes to see! I thank you for the Blood for I have been redeemed. You are my light in the darkness, my strength when I am weak. You're amazing Lord! Thank you God*

When she couldn't sing anymore she fell to her knees with the rest of the congregation and worshipped and praised God. Pastor was kneeling, crying, and praising God as well.

God was pleased with her and enjoyed being in the midst of their worship. He showered them with the Holy Ghost and deliver many from sickness, cast out the spirit of fear, laziness, poverty, low self esteem and so much more. Everyone from young to old began to speak in the spirit. Church Of Christ will never be the same again.

It took awhile for service to get back under control. Pastor had to recover and thank God. Of all his years he has never felt the Holy Ghost so strong before.

Once service was over Sabrina, Mother Mary, Sherry and Zachariah were standing around talking.

"God is so good! God bless you Sabrina for letting the Lord use you. You have no idea how many lives you touched. Lord, I didn't know you could sing like that." Mother Mary says with bright eyes.

"I can hold a note but I have never sang in front of people before, nor preach. That was all God and not me. It felt great though." Sabrina says with a smile.

"Well He definitely used you honey. I haven't cried and praised God that much and so hard since I was first introduced to God. You were there. You really blessed me just like last time. I feel like a new woman." Sherry says.

"Thank God not me. Speaking of introductions. Sherry this is Zachariah, Zach this is my best friend Sherry." Sabrina says to Zach.

"Hello Sherry, it is a pleasure to meet you" Zach replied extending his hand for a hand shake.

Sherry reach for his hand and when she touched it a cool breeze and the smell of fresh flowers surrounded her.

"My Lord, you really are heaven sent!" She says staring in his eyes still holding his hand.

Mother Mary and Sabrina laughed. Sherry lets go of his hand and rolls her eyes.

"It's not in a flirtatious way. A blind man can see he is anointed. Let me go home, see, this is how rumors start in the church." she says cutting her eyes at everyone.

"No, I truly understand what you mean Sherry. I have to tell you. God says for you to stay on this path. Stay close to Sabrina as Ruth to Naomi, for your blessing will come." Zach said to her.

Sherry looked at Sabrina and Sabrina at Sherry and they both smiled at each other with love in their hearts for one another. They were more like sisters than friends.

"Yes Sir, only death can keep me from it! Me and you must never part" She sang while imitating the hand moves from the Color Purple. They all busted out laughing.

"Girl get your silly self out of here!" Mother Mary says smiling and waving her away.

"Okay, but serious, I won't leave her. Bye you guys, have a blessed night." Sherry says as she gives Mother Mary a hug and kiss as well as Sabrina.

"Sabrina! Bless you for that word Woman of God. If I didn't know any better I'd think you might be trying to take my job. That was a blessing and right on time." Pastor says to Sabrina as he joins the group and shakes her hand.

"Oh no Pastor, that was a one time thing unless I am called to ministry. Then that will be something I will have to pray about. I can't say no to the Lord but I will make sure he calls me if that is what he wants. It was truly all God's doing." Sabrina says with a smile

"Well, I think you were just called. We will see what God says though. Just my opinion." Pastor says.

Sabrina looked at him shocked. "Thank you Pastor" she says with another big smile.

Mother Mary was watching and smiling as they talked in total agreement with her son.

"Brother Zach. May I speak with you in my office?" He said looking at Zach.

"Sure, excuse us ladies." Zach replied and they both walked away.

"So child how are you? That word and praise you gave was amazing. God is truly calling you to something." Mother says to Sabrina.

"I am still floating and in awe at God. To use me and bless me like He has been doing. It's a place I never want to leave." Sabrina says.

"Oh, child you don't know how blessed you are. Still, with every blessing there comes a storm. Don't let your guard down yet." Mother replied.

"No Ma'am I won't. I am just grateful for the things he is doing for me now and will do. Even through the storms I will still bless his name." Sabrina says with pride.

Mother Mary smiles. *Yes child, you will make a great wife for my son. Thank you God.* Mother Mary thinks to herself.

"Okay baby, I have to go, you take care and remember if you need me just give me a call." Mother says giving her a hug.

"Yes ma'am. I remember, love you!" Sabrina says.

"I love you too sweetie" says mother.

Mother watched Sabrina try to get through the crowd. She noticed that most people looked at her as the First Lady. She waved and gave hugs to everyone as she left. Today was just a taste and a test of what the world would soon receive when all this was over. Talk about an anointed couple. *Lord please tell me when you will open there eyes to see each other.*

When Sabrina made it home Max was asleep on the couch with his shirt off, and his hand in his unzipped pants. She cleaned up all the beer bottles and he turned his head to the left revealing a hickey on his neck. Sabrina just stared at it for a while. Not sure how to feel. What kind of woman would come to a married man's house and sleep with him while she was at church. Then to leave evidence truly showed she was nothing but a jezebel. No respect for herself or anyone else. Sabrina went to the kitchen throwing the empty bottles in the trash a little too hard.

Calming herself down she prayed "Lord, I know you are working. I don't want to care about what he does anymore. It hurts and he doesn't deserve my feelings or the hurt. Take this pain away from me Lord. In Jesus name Amen! Just like the devil to try and steal your joy when you're winning the fight. You won't win Satan! I bind you in this fight now in the name of Jesus. I am taking my joy back in Jesus name Amen."

Chapter 11
Help me

Pastor

Pastor went into his office with Zach and locked the door. He honestly didn't know where to start or what to say. He was still thinking about the message that Sabrina gave tonight. Wow! He thought. She was amazing and God was amazing for giving her the message that he needed to hear. He could not have delivered it better himself.

"Have a seat Zach, would you like a water? I don't know about you but my throat is dry. I haven't felt the power of God move like that before in all my years of preaching." Pastor says as he gets two waters out of the refrigerator for them.

"Sure, I could use one myself. Sabrina is a wonderful woman of God and will do great things here." Zach says to Pastor looking for any sign of attraction toward Sabrina but there was none. Just the love of Christ. No lust. Just admiration for the body of Christ. *Lord, how do you shield a man's true wife from him and she is so close to him?* He questioned in his mind to God.

IT IS NOT THEIR TIME YET. THEY HAVE TO COMPLETE THIS TEST BEFORE I CAN OPEN THEIR EYES TO TRULY SEE EACH OTHER. WHAT I HAVE IN STORE FOR THEM NO MAN OR PRINCIPALITIES CAN BREAK BUT I HAVE TO MAKE SURE THEY ARE READY FOR THE RESPONSIBILITIES AND GIFTS. THEY ARE ALMOST THERE. God says to Zach.

"Yeah she is. I tell you sometimes I don't know what I would do without her here. If it wasn't for Sabrina and my mother I would be a lost puppy. She even takes on the duty of the First Lady when my wife isn't available. Which has been more often lately. It's funny some of the people that don't attend here sometimes think that she is my wife. She is always available for God's work. She will be blessed for it for sure." Pastor says thinking about his next words.

"Yes she will be." Zach replied knowing a lot more than Pastor could ever imagine.

"Speaking of my wife. I don't know how to say this but God told me to speak with you. There seems to be some trouble in my personal life and with me being the Pastor I can't just talk to anyone. Since God sent me to you I can trust this stays between us?" Pastor asked.

"Oh yes, I am a man of my word. It is not in my nature to gossip or lie. This will stay between us." Zach informed him.

"Well about a year and a half ago my wife began to get sick more often than normal. I noticed that she was only sick on the days we had church or some kind of event. Sundays and of course Tuesday nights. Tonight of course she didn't have to provide a excuse, I didn't ask her to come. The thing is when I make it home she is fully dressed, not home or fresh out the shower with makeup on or on her way back home. She admits to cheating but won't tell me with who. I need to have her followed and I need a background check on her. She says I don't really know who she is and that she could make my life hell if I try to divorce her. She only wants to stay for my money. I don't want that nor do I want the congregation to find out about this. Church people can be very unforgiving as well as hurtful sometimes. They tend to forget about the word forgiveness when their feelings are hurt. I don't want God to lose one soul that is saved over my mess. You know what I mean?" Pastor informed Zach.

"I am sorry you are going through this Pastor and I will do all that I can to help. Once I give you the information I want you to stay focused on God. Don't look to the left nor to the right. But only unto him. God makes no mistake we are the ones that fall when things get a little rocky." Zachariah says to him.

"I am trying but even preachers have bad days Zach" Pastor says as he rubs his hand over his head in frustration.

"I know try to think of it this way. You are driving to get to a certain destination. You look up ahead and you see you are about to drive right into a storm. You know that it's about to get bad so you start to get ready. You pray and ask God for help to get you through it. The mist starts to fall and you look to your left. You see the sun in the distance and you wish you were over there. The rain gets harder and the wind blows. Your car starts to shake and you feel the car slipping to the left. You almost lost control of the car because you looked back at the Sunshine. You're scared and you want to stop and pull over until the storm ends but you know you are pressed for time. So you pray to God. You keep your eyes straight ahead and you focus. You cut off all distractions and you remain in control of the car. Soon the rain and the wind slows back down to just a drizzle. The sun starts to peek through the clouds and a rainbow appears. God's promise and blessings are on the way. You made it. You just have to stay focused on Him and not the world. A test of faith and courage is getting you right where He needs you to be." Zach explains to Pastor.

"Wow, ok I see where you're going with this. So I am not where God wants me to be so I have to go through this storm to get the blessings that He has for me? Okay no problem, but why does the storm have to be so big and strong you know?" Asked Pastor.

"Well, if he gave you light rains you wouldn't learn from it. How would God know who truly loves him if no one had to prove it. Free will was a blessing and a curse. Anyone can drive in rain, but a storm, that is focus, faith and dedication. If we were in the times of Adam and Eve, I would love it, but we are not and because of their mistakes we have to be very careful not to fall from his grace. Thank God it's not as easy to do nowadays as it was back then. Thanks to Jesus that is." Zach smiles.

"That makes sense!" Pastor says.

"Yeah, if we didn't have free will would God truly have people that love and serve him?" Zach asked.

"Well, I guess not. They would do it only because it's all they knew and had to do." Pastor says with confusion on his face

"He gave us free will for a reason, his ways are beyond our thinking but God has good reason for the things He does. You can't truly help someone if you have never been through what they are going through. You can give your advice and opinions but that is all. Jesus had to come and be flesh in order to save us. He had to feel what we felt, resist temptation and see what we see everyday. He became sin in order to save us from it." Zach says.

"Wow you are truly a great man of God. No wonder God sent me to you. It's not too often that I get to speak with another man of God and not have to pray for them. Would it be ok if we exchanged numbers for when I need a second opinion on things I don't understand?" Pastor asks reaching for his phone.

"Sure. I don't get out much being new in town I could use some brotherly love." Zach says.

They exchange numbers and head for the door.

"Do you know how long it will be before I can get the information. I am kind of sleeping here at the church.

"I have the perfect man that can help me with this, give me a day for background and two for her to be followed.

"Cool the sooner the better I have to figure somethings out." replied Pastor.
"No problem at all, before I leave do you mind if I pray for you?" asked Zack.

"Of course not, Pastors need more prayer than others." Pastor said smiling.

"I know, you guys are under attack more than anyone. Satan wants to stop you from speaking the word of God by any means necessary." Zach says.

Zach put one hand on Pastor's shoulder and the other in his hand and bowed his head. As soon as they bowed their heads the spirits of anger, confusion, unforgiveness, bitterness, and fear started to scream. "Lord I am here with your son Jonathan and we come to you as humble as we know how. I ask that you cover Pastor Jonathan, keep him strong in your faith for what's to come. Lord, I cast down every evil spirit that is not like you Lord and I cast them into the pits of hell from where them come. Spirit of jealousy, hate, fear, confusion, unforgiveness, rejection and loneliness. You have no place here and I command you in the name of Jesus to leave now! Lord we thank you for the trials and tribulation. We know there is victory after the battle. Even when it gets hard and we don't understand it. Lord, no weapon form against him shall prosper. *For we wrestle not against flesh and blood but against principalities, against powers, the rulers of darkness of this world, against spiritual wickedness in high places. Ephesians 6:12 tells us.* Thank you for staying with us Lord and never leaving our sides. In Jesus name Amen!"

As Zach prayed the evil spirits fell off Pastor kicking and screaming into the pits of hell. Pastor heard the Voice of the Lord say.

"STAY WITH ME SON, THE STORM IS COMING." God whispered to them.

"Yes Father I will" They both replied and looked at each other.

"Did you hear him too" Pastor asked.

"Yes, everything will be okay. Always remember you're not alone." Zach says.

"I'll never forget that again Thank you brother" Pastor says with a big smile.

Chapter 12
What's done in the dark

Max

Max laid in his bed after eating his breakfast. He couldn't stop thinking about those shoes and how she walked out of this house knowing he did not agree with her choice of clothing. *Who is she trying to impress at that church, is it that new accountant? She must think I am stupid to believe that Sherry bought those shoes. That's an eight hundred dollar pair of shoes. Only a man that wants something from her would buy those. If she is cheating she is disgusting sleeping with people for material things. That is just low and she has no respect for me or herself. It's ok, I have a trick for her.*

He got up and searched through her closet for the shoes and any clothes that were either too tight or revealing. She didn't have but a few things that were too tight and those shoes were her only pair that he considered sexy. He got some matches from the kitchen drawer and took the clothes outside placing them into their outside fireplace.

"I won't burn the shoes, I will give them to Tonya, she likes stuff like this. Maybe this will change her mind in getting that money. This will teach Sabrina to listen to me" He says talking to himself.

He lit a match and as he dropped it into the fire the wind blew and the match went out before it touched the clothing. He tried again but this time used his hand as a shield to stop the wind. That didn't work the wind just blew harder. The third time he went into the house and found some old mail. He lit it and tried to cover it from the wind but the wind blew it out again. He tried the fourth time and the matches would not light. Frustrated with the wind he took the clothes in the house and into the bathroom. He ran down the hall into the laundry room to get some bleach. He got the brand new one and headed to the bathroom. He placed the clothes into the tub and lifted the bottle and started to pour but nothing came out. Scared and confused he dropped the bleach on the bathroom floor and the bleach spilled everywhere.

"Ok Max, stop tripping" he coached himself.

To test his theory he picked up the bleach swished it around in his hand and poured some on the floor.

"Yeah you tripping Max" He laughs at himself.

As he lifted the bottle again his hand began to get warm and as he tilted the bottle to pour again nothing came out and his hand instantly felt like it was on fire.

"Awwwwww, what the hell is going on?" He screams at no one in particular running the to toilet to stick his hand in so the cold water could stop the burning. His hand even made a sizzling sound when it touched the water. When he took his hand out of the toilet and looked at his hand it was perfectly normal. No burn, no redness, just his hand. Looking around the room he saw that the bleach is still spilling out of the bottle onto the floor.

"There is some crazy bewitched stuff going on. Did she put curse on me or something? I need a drink" He says frustrated, scared and confused. *Cursed be he that taketh reward to slay an innocent person. And all the people shall say, Amen. Deuteronomy 27:25 KJV* Max slightly heard this verse as he looked around the bathroom.

"Sabrina can clean this mess up later." He says to afraid to touch the bottle again.

He picks up the shoes grabs his keys and leaves to get a drink and some food. Looking over at the shoes in the passenger seat he calls Tonya.

"Hey baby, what you doing?" He says as she picks up the phone.

"Nothing what's up" she replies dryly.

"Meet me at the Cheesecake Factory. I have something for you." He says to her.

"Oh really? Okay, I'll be there in twenty minutes. I am hungry." she says excited.

"You always hungry bye" He says and hangs up the phone.

Once he makes it to the restaurant 30 minutes later. He grabbed the shoes and walks in just as Tonya was being seated. She looked beautiful as usual to him but he knew this was just an outer appearance. She was a wolf in sheep's clothing. So he went and sat in front of her and placed the shoes on the table.

"Here you go baby." he says as he waits for her response.

"Oh wow, you went all out for me. I love this brand of shoes. Of course I can only buy a pair two or three times a year. I love these! They are beautiful thank you" She says smiling.

"You're welcome! It was no problem you deserve it." He says rubbing his hand.

"Are you ok you look nervous and you keep rubbing your hand." She says looking at him weird.

"I am fine, let's just get our food to go, it's too many people in here." he says looking around. He had a feeling someone was watching him. As he looked behind him he saw Sherry coming their way with two people he didn't know. The waiter had just brought there drink orders to the table.

"Aww hell" he says under his breath.

"What's wrong Max?" Tonya asked.

"Sabrina's best friend Sherry is headed this way just be cool." He says to her.

Tonya just rolled her eyes. She didn't care that Sherry was there Pastor already knew she was cheating and she felt she had nothing to worry about. Besides they are just having a conversation. As Sherry was being escorted to her table she noticed Tonya but not Max yet.

"Oh, Hi First Lady Tonya, How have you been? Oh my, hi Max this is a pleasant surprise. You two go ahead I will find you in a minute." She says to her clients surprised to see them together without their spouses. Looking at the table Sherry noticed the box that looked similar to the box of shoes she bought Sabrina a few years back. She also noticed that both of them had alcohol beverages from the 3 o'clock happy hour drink special. It's why she brings her clients to celebrate the closing of their houses. Although she only has a half a glass of wine for herself. Her clients tend to enjoy it.

"So what brings you two here?" Sherry asks as her clients are seated a few seats away. *Thank you God I am saved, a few months ago this would turn out bad for them. I know they think I am stupid.* She thinks to herself.

Max not sure what to say looks at Tonya to respond.

"Oh just doing God's work as usual. Sabrina wanted to gift me with these shoes being that she was at work she asked Max to bring them to me see, aren't the wonderful. Now we are just getting a bite to eat and talking about God." She says showing Sherry the shoes she bought for her best friend.

"Oh yes they are wonderful. They look like something I would pick out for myself. Someone has good taste in shoes don't you think Max?" Tonya says staring at him as if she could kill him with her eyes.

"Yes, they are amazing but not Sabrina's taste of shoes, That's why she gave them to Tonya." He says agreeing with her but praying this doesn't backfire on him.

"Yeah, I guess you know her better than me, So since you guys are here doing God's work I guess I will be seeing the both of you in church come Sunday. You know we have missed you both for quite some time. Oh, and you should wear the shoes, I am sure Sabrina would love to see you in them." She replies trying her best to calm down and be nice. *There is no way I am not telling my friend about this. I know for a fact she would never give those shoes away. She was just able to wear them yesterday at church.* She says in her mind.

"If it's in God's will, I will be there. You know people are dying and getting sick left and right now a days. You should be careful too you know." Tonya replied in a warning voice.

"Yes, I know the devil is busy, but God is great and mighty. *A lion which is strongest among beasts, and turneth not way for any (P*roverbs 30;30) See you around First Lady." She says with attitude and walks away. Not even caring to address Max.

"Now, why would you tell her Sabrina gave you these shoes? You know they are best friends and she is going to ask her!" Max whispers with anger rising in his voice.

"Well what would you have liked me to say. I came to meet my sidepiece for brunch and to get my gift he bought me. You know Sabrina will not say anything to you about it she is too scared of you." she says annoyed that he was even worried at all.

"Yeah, you're right, I just don't need the headache" he say thinking about how he might be cursed and that if she did say something to him he wouldn't be able to say or do anything about it anyway.

"Let's just get our food and go. I have to talk with you in private about some things anyway." Tonya say to him. Plotting on how she was going to get Pastor's money and leave town.

Chapter 13
You won't believe this.

Sherry

Sherry sat in that restaurant with her clients trying her hardest to stay focused. She rushed her clients to sign the last of their paperwork and excused herself. Apologizing to her clients for not staying to celebrate with them she left a hundred dollars on the table to cover their meals and drinks. Her clients were so happy about the house they didn't even notice her change of attitude and were fine with her leaving. They were newlyweds so they wanted to be alone anyway. Tonya and Max had already left and she was happy about it. If she saw them again she wasn't sure she would be able to control herself again.

She parked her car in her usual parking space. Right next to Sabrina's. Happy that she was still in her office she had to tell her what she saw. What kind of friend would she be if she didn't say anything. *I knew he was going to get back at her for wearing those shoes.* She thinks to herself angrily pushing the elevator button. She just didn't think that he would give them away. On top of that he gives them to someone she knows and sees often at church. Well, she used to see her often. It's been a long time since Tonya was at church. *"They're not Sabrina's taste of shoes!"* She mimics to herself in her head as the elevator doors open. *No they are not your taste of shoes, you want my best friend to walk around like a Muslim and you are not even a Muslim. You eat pork chops like it's the last supper. Jesus, take the wheel! Calm down girl! You have to be cool for Sabrina.*

I can't stand for a man to have a good woman and treat her like crap. I knew he was abusive to her sometimes but to cheat too and with the Pastor's wife. Lord have mercy. Pastor is going to be crushed after all he did for Max when he first came to the church. This is a big mess. Lord how do I tell my friend what I just saw. Will she believe me? Will she get mad at me and say I am making things up. She has been so happy lately so maybe she already knows. Sherry's mind was in overdrive and she was not sure how to tell Sabrina at all. She reached Sabrina's office and said a prayer.

"Lord, I said that I would never intervene in my friend's marriage but what they are doing is wrong and she needs to know. Please don't let her be mad at me Lord. Please let her believe me God. I will die for this woman. I love her like she is my blood sister, be with me and her through this storm. In Jesus name Amen!" She knocked on the door and waited.

"Come in please." Sabrina says in her sweet work voice.

"Oh, Hey girl, what's up I was just finishing up. How did it go? Was the couple happy?" Sabrina asked confused that her friend was not happy after she closed a million dollar contract.

"Yes, they were very happy, so was the other couple I saw." Sherry says sadly and under her breath.

"Oh so why the long face?" Sherry asked concerned.

"Sabrina, sit down I have to tell you something. Before I tell you I need you to know something about my past." She says with tears in her eyes. She loves Sabrina so much that if her friend was hurt she was too and she hates she has to be the one to give her this information. A real friend never wants to bring bad news to their friend.

"Okay, you're scaring me but I will listen sit down." Sabrina replied sitting in her seat and motioning for Sherry to do the same across from her.

"Okay, a few years before I got this job my best friend was in a very abusive marriage. I saw her get beat up by her husband a couple times and I would always help her but she would always go back to him because they had children. Anyway, she finally got tired of the cheating and fighting and asked me to come get her and the kids. He had went out drinking with his friends and wouldn't be back until later so we thought we had enough time. He came back earlier than expected and when he got there he was really drunk. He didn't say anything to her he just looked at her crazy and all the bags and went to the kids room. I begged her to just leave the stuff grab the kids and we would figure the rest out later. She was so scared that he didn't say anything and thought he was going to get his gun so she pushed me out the door and made me leave. I hung around for about an hour then I called to police. It was too quiet for my comfort. Once the police checked it out they said everything was fine. The kids were sleep and so was he. So I went home. I still had a bad feeling about her being there with him. Well, the police didn't check the kids good enough because he had suffocated the kids in their sleep while she was pushing me out the door. My friend didn't know. When she peeked in on them through the door they looked to be sleeping. He played sleep until the police left and she laid down. He shot her in the head and then shot himself right next to her. I heard about it on the news the next morning. Someone heard the gunshots and called the police. One of the neighbors said they stayed up because he was known to beat up his wife on the weekends and if he heard anything he was going to do something about it this time. We were both too late. I vowed to never intervene in another person's marriage that way again."

"Oh my Lord, Sherry, I am so sorry." Sabrina said crying her eyes out.

"I blamed myself for so long. I keep thinking maybe if I would have fought her harder to stay, or called the police sooner than I could have stopped it. God works in mysterious ways. When I won my rape case I donated ten percent to the church. When Pastor saw the amount he called me into the office and asked me about it. It's because of me that the church has God's Helping Hands women's shelter. I requested that he use some of the money to start A.C.E. Legaci Foundation LLC. I teach abuse awareness classes on the weekends and spend a lot of my free time just talking and hanging with the women and children. No one knows that most of the proceeds come from me. They think it's from the church. I didn't want to be the CEO of if but Pastor insisted. He and the board members are the only ones that know who I am. Most people think I just love to volunteer. I don't want anyone to know I am a millionaire, because of the case. I like to stay in the background." Sherry says shyly.

"Oh, my Lord, I had no idea. That is wonderful that you do that for so many people. I had no idea. I thought you went out every weekend to party. So what does this have to do with me?" Sabrina laughs nervously knowing what her friend was about to say.

Sherry takes a deep breath "Sabrina I know that Max is abusive to you. You are the best at hiding it. I will give you that. It took awhile for me to see it at first. I was hoping you would come to me so I could help you. After you preached last night the mentioning of the shoes and what I saw today I figured you were in your early phases of leaving and you would come to me. But then I saw something at the restaurant and I knew I had to tell you." Sherry says getting angry all over again.

"What did you see today?" Sabrina asked.

"You know I take most of my clients to The Cheesecake Factory to celebrate the closing of a house. While I was there I saw your husband Max with a woman. Not just any woman but Tonya. Pastor's wife! He gave her your shoes you had on last night that I bought you. She had the nerve to say that you gifted them to her because they were not your style. Max was kind enough to bring them to her so they decided to get some food and have drinks while doing the "Lord's work" so they say she said using finger quotation marks with her hands as she said "Lords work." "Can you believe it? It took every cell that God has in me not to act a fool in there. I wouldn't be your friend if I didn't tell you. Especially when I know you love those shoes!" She says looking at her friend as tears roll down her face and she starts to cry.

Sabrina was crying so hard that she was almost yelling. Sherry got up and held her friend in her arms as she lets out all of her hurt and pain. Now that she has told her what now. Sabrina stops crying after about five minutes looks at her friend and smiles.

"Thank you, I have been holding that in for a long time." Sabrina says as she cleans her face with tissue that Sherry got her in the midst of her crying.

"It's ok, what are friends for. How many times have you let me cry on your shoulder. You are always so strong. You hold everything in and try to please everybody. What about you and your happiness. You deserve to be truly happy. Not just on the outside but the inside as well. Why didn't you tell me? You have no idea how many times I praised God that you walked in this office every morning. I was so scared for you. I was scared that if I asked you would push me away and tell me to stay out of your business." Sherry says as she wipes her own tears.

"I was ashamed, scared, fearful of what you might think of me. You come to me for help, how could I have come to you for help. For so long you and God were the only happiness I had and I didn't want to ruin it with my problems." Sabrina says to her friend sitting back in her chair.

"You remember what Zach said. You're my Naomi and I am your Ruth. I will not leave you no matter what. So what do we do about Max?" Sherry asked.

"I don't know, God has been working it out so far but this is crazy. Tonya of all people, no wonder she has an attitude when I come around. I thought she was thinking I might want her man but she has been sleeping with mine. It makes perfect sense now. They are never at church anymore. She has been to my house this week too. We used to be so close" Sabrina says angrily.

"She what! How do you know that? Never mind don't answer that. We can do this like we don't have a saved bone in our body or we can go the Godly way. What you think? That demon threatened me today too. She thinks I didn't catch it. Sabrina girl, you would have been so proud of me. I hit her with a Bible verse and walked away." Sherry says with confidence and anger.

"Good, then you remember the verse be angry and sin not?" Sabrina laughed even while her heart was breaking her friend could always makes her smile. It's hard to find friends like that now a days.

"Yeah, yeah I remember. That one was always one that was the hardest for me to follow. Can I suggest something. Can you not go back to that house. I know that is hard to do but I promise I got you. I have a rental property in Greenville that I use when I stay there. I also rent it out on Airbnb. It is empty and you can stay there as long as you want. I can
take you shopping and we can get you some clothes and toiletries until we can get your stuff?" Sherry asked hopeful that she would say yes.

"I could use a break from the stress. Yes I'll go. I am pretty sure my marriage is over anyway. I asked God for a way out so I would be stupid not to take it right?" Sabrina smiles and feels like a weight have been lifted off her shoulders.

"I wouldn't say stupid just not smart, ya know?" They both laughed.

"Okay. Let me go finish up so we can get out of here. I am about to buy you a whole new wardrobe. Finally, we are going to see the real Sabrina" Sherry says excited.

Sabrina just laughed at her friend. She planned to pay for her own clothing. Sabrina wasn't rich like Sherry but she could afford a new wardrobe. They both finished up the last of their filing and record keeping and a hour later they were headed to the mall.

Chapter 14
The plot

Tonya

Tonya drove to their usual hotel the Drury Inn on Woodruff Road and checked in for the night. She had a feeling that her husband was not going to be home no time soon so why not make a night of it. He wouldn't even know she thought. Once inside the room they sat in silence.

"So I have been trying to figure out how we can get in the accountant room and make it look like the new accountant is stealing and not us." She says looking at Max.

"Okay I am listening." Max says.

"Well I know that he just got here but I think I have it figured out. Sabrina came to see him around lunch time on Monday. I didn't think anything of it but we can use that in our favor. We will have to both attend church Sunday."

"Why? What do you mean she visited him at lunch on Monday?" Max asked getting angry.

"Well she didn't say why nor did I ask, you remember when I told you when I met him I got all hot and not in a good way?" She says trying to explain and make it worse than it was.

"Well, when I ran out of there and Jonathan came after me. They stayed behind. I don't know how long she was with him I just know they didn't come check on me." she says to him.

"She did come home happier than usual that day." Max says thinking about that day in detail.

"Yeah well, I was thinking if you come to church accusing him of sleeping with your wife I can slip into the office and plant a letter from Tamika. It is going to be a bunch of lies about how Zach was her pimp and he came to the church to take her place because she had a change of heart from stealing from the church. She is going to be asking the Pastor for forgiveness and exposing Zach instead of me and you." Tonya said with a smile.

"That's not a bad idea at all. That way I can let off some steam." He replies with an evil grin.

"After the letter is planted, depending on if my husband tries to divorce me because I am cheating. I can spread lies about him being in on it and a number of other things that I have in mind. I will get my money and we can leave this place. Just me and you and start over somewhere else." She said in a seductive way that made Max smile.

"Sounds like a great plan baby." Max said excited in more ways than one.

She got up to close the windows as Max wrapped his arms around her to kiss the back of her neck. Both of them not knowing that Zachariah was disguised as someone else taking pictures. He has been following her all day. He has seen all that he needed to see to talk to Pastor Jonathan. Now, they just needed the background report.

Chapter 15
War in the Natural

Sabrina

Sabrina and Sherry shopped until the mall closed. She thought that it was funny that
Max had not called her to see where she was. She knows that dinner is always done by
seven o'clock every day. I guess it's a good thing though. She really didn't want to
answer his calls nor was she going to. She was officially in hiding. Herself and Sherry
were just pulling up to the house she was going to be calling her new home for a while.
"Oh my Lord!" Sabrina say as she pulls in to a three car garage home. The house was
made of brick with its own private gate for security. You literally had to buzz yourself in.
Once they parked and got out she looked at Sherry and said.

"Are you sure we are at the right house. This is too big for just me. I would be scared to
stay here alone."

'Oh don't worry about that, I am not leaving you here alone for quite some time. Not until
we know you are safe. If I do have to leave I have security cameras and he can't get
past the gate unless you let him in. I also have motion detectors around the yard. Plus
he doesn't know where this place is anyway. You are completely safe. Trust me." Sherry
replied with a smile.

"Are you a spy or something too?" Sabrina asked very serious. You only see this type of
security in movies.

"Girl no. I originally got this place for women that had husbands and kids that went
through extreme measures to get them back but I haven't had to use it for that until now.
I do have guns in here and I do have a black belt in Karate. After I was raped I vowed to
never be a victim again." Sherry replied laughing.

"Okay I see you, my own personal bodyguard too, I see you God! My Ruth is the truth
and has nothing on the Bible Ruth." Sherry laughs excited to learn all this about her
friend.

"I will be teaching you a few pointers as well, so I hope you're ready for a one on one
self defense session." Sherry looked at her friend with a serious face.

"Of course I am ready, I have always wanted to take those classes but Max wouldn't let me." Sabrina says sadly grabbing more bags out of the car.

"Well, all that is over now. Welcome to the new you!" She says opening the front door.

"Oh my Lord Sherry, This is beautiful! You sure you want me to stay here. I can stay in a hotel or something. You don't have to do this" she says about to cry. Sherry wants her to stay in a mini mansion and she bought her a brand new wardrobe. She spent ten thousand dollars on her and now this. It was truly a blessing.

"Girl come on in this house, let me show you your room first, and then I will give you a tour. We still have to get the rest of the bags out of the car. I'll order a pizza while we unpack."

"Girl, how much do you rent this place out for? Is that a swimming pool in the back? How many rooms?" Sabrina asked as she looked around following Sherri to the elevator. "You have a elevator in this house Sherry? Do you know how many great girl's nights we could have had, I am so mad. I knew you had money but I didn't know it was like this." Sabrina says excited.

"$3,000 a day, yes that is a swimming pool. It also has a Jacuzzi, basketball court, gym, and an in home movie theater. We are about to have a blast." Sherry says laughing at her friend.

"Yasssss, this is the best hideout place I have ever seen." Sabrina says.

"Thanks!" Sherry says dragging the bags into the bedroom.

Looking around she had a big king size bed, her own personal bathroom, a balcony in the bedroom overlooking the pool. The color of the walls were white and the carpet was beige. Red and cream curtains that match the bed cover and the dresser were also red and creme. The bathroom even had the same color scheme.

"I call this my strawberries and cream room" Sherry says laughing.

"It is beautiful. I can't thank you enough. I have a question. If you have all this why stay in the one bedroom home when you can live anywhere?" Sabrina asked curious about her friend.

"Well, for one it's just me, there is no need for all of this with no family. Two, I don't want people to know I have all this. It tends to change them. Three, it's just material things. I can't take it to heaven with me. I would rather share it with the less fortunate. I plan to be one of the rich people that actually make it into heaven" Sherry says in a matter of fact kind of way.

"I completely understand, I am not rich like you but I am far from poor, I have close to a million in my separate bank account that Max doesn't know about. My mama didn't raise no fool when it came to money. She would always say to me, *Chile Proverbs 31 in the Bible it says the wife worked just as hard as the man and had a business of her own. Don't be depending on no man financially to take care of you.*" Sabrina says in her mother's voice. They both laughed and headed to the car to get more bags.

"Mama was a smart woman I see!" Sherry says.

"Yeah she was." Sabrina says smiling thinking her mama would be proud of her now for leaving Max. They made four more tips to the car to get all the items. While Sabrina organized her things. Sherry ordered a large meat lovers pizza and Pepsi. After they ate Sabrina asked Sherry.

"So you're the expert on this domestic violence stuff, what's the next move?" Sabrina asked.

"Well being that it is 9 o'clock and he hasn't called he hasn't realized that you have left yet. My guess is they are still together and he hasn't made it home. So I would be looking for his call in the morning. My guess is he might send you a message saying he will be out late or nothing at all. He thinks you are home waiting for him. After he calls don't pick up the phone under any circumstances he will try to sweet talk you into coming back. Being that this is your first time leaving it might be a little easy to do, no offense." Sherry says.

"None taken" Sabrina laughs.

"When he can't reach you he will start to look for you because he knows all of your places you usually are including work. I recommend you work from here. We can talk to the manager and let her know. I have a fax machine so she can fax you everything you need. Don't worry she knows that I help women and she loves you so she will have no issue with this at all." Sherry explains.

"Ok Cool!" Sabrina says.

"When he starts looking for you he will be angry, so we need to get you a restraining order and have it served to him so he knows that you have left for sure. Today is Wednesday so I can have him served by Friday. After that, you file for a divorce and live a happy blessed life." Sherry finishes.

"Well that sound good and easy, but knowing Max this is going to get bad when he can't find me. He will know you know where I am. He might even try to follow you" Sabrina says.

"No worries. I am licensed to carry and remember I have a black belt in karate. I can give Jet Li a run for his money. Not only that, we have the best defense ever created." Sherry says smiling from ear to ear.

"Oh yeah, what's that?"

"Girl you should know, you introduced me to him..... God and he does not play about his children 1 Chronicles 1:22 *touch not mine anointed and do my prophets not harm.* That was a warning honey and you my dear friend are anointed by God" Sherry says smiling.

"Yeah, you are right about that" Sabrina smiles thinking of the oil in her bag.

"So just relax for a change and enjoy being free. I will make some phone calls in the morning and we can do some work then have a relaxing day by the pool. I would recommend getting a new phone number but I know everyone has this number so for now just block his number after he starts to blow your phone up in the am." Sherry tells her.

"Okay, sounds great" she says getting up to go to her room for sleep.

Hey, before you go to bed let's pray together!" Sherry says walking toward Sabrina.

"Ok" Sabrina says.

"Follow me, we can use my prayer closet. You are welcome to use this room whenever you want ok."

"Thank you I'll put it to good use." Sabrina reassures her.

Sabrina followed Sherry down the hall and stopped under the staircase. She opens the door and there was a small room the size of a half bathroom. A window to let natural light in and a windowsill with pillows in it. On both sides were candles and incense. They both went in and Sherry lit the candles and incense. They got on their knees and faced each other holding hands. Sherry began to pray. "Lord, you said where two or three are gathered in your name you will be in the midst of it. Well, we are here and we need your help, strength and guidance now. We know there is a spiritual war that you are working on Sabrina's behalf but we need help in the natural war. Lord the enemy will come and try to take what he thinks belongs to him, I bind him right now in the name of Jesus and I plead the blood of Jesus over my friend Sabrina as well as myself. No weapon formed against us shall prosper. Lord, we know that weapons may form but we believe they won't be able to prosper Lord. Keep your hand on her Lord. Thank you for never leaving her Father in Jesus name Amen" Sherry finishes her prayer but Sabrina starts hers.

"Lord we give you all honor, glory and praise, Lord you are amazing and I thank you for sending me this angel. My friend Sherry. Lord you gave her to me as a friend for such a time as this Lord and I thank you so much. All the things I have prayed for you have blessed me with and I am beyond grateful, Lord. I thank you in advance for what is to come. I ask for strength and courage to face each day until I can get my divorce. I know it won't be easy but we have the best fighter on our side and that is you. So continue to fight with us in the spiritual realm and the natural. For whatever I bind in heaven shall be bound in earth and whatever I loose in heaven shall be loose in earth. Lord we bind the hands of the enemy that has come to steal, kill and destroy Lord and we cancel it right now in the name of Jesus. I thank you for the angels that you have sent my way for protection God. I know that it is because of you that I am alive. I know that I have a purpose to fulfill in the Kingdom or I wouldn't be here. Lord, I am here and I am ready! Use me as you will Father and bless Sherry for all the things that she does. Not just for me but for everyone. In Jesus name Amen.

A chill ran through the girls and God whispered to Sherry
"I AM PLEASED WITH YOU AND YOU WILL BE BLESSED. DON'T LEAVE HER, SHE IS THE KEY TO YOUR BLESSING"

"SABRINA, STAY STRONG DAUGHTER. IT WILL BE OVER SOON I HAVE MANY PLANS FOR YOU MY CHILD" God says to Sabrina and leaves the room.

The girls began to speak in the spirit and praise God until they couldn't praise him anymore. They were drunk in the spirit and they fell asleep in the prayer closet.

Chapter 16
She has lost her mind

Max

Max got home after 10 in the morning. He didn't feel like being bothered or questioned about where he was because he was going to be leaving in about a week anyway. As soon as this plan worked out. Tonya and Max planned to move to Mexico and never return. What can he say, he loved them both. Sabrina and Tonya were completely opposite. If he could put them together to make one woman he would be a happy man. He walked into their room and got in the shower. He made him some breakfast which he thought was strange that she didn't make it before work. *I guess she figured no need to since I wasn't home. I'll let that one slide since I was out all night.* He thought to himself. As he was walking past the laundry room he kept smelling something strong. Looking into the bathroom he saw the mess he left with the clothes he tried to bleach. It was still there and the fumes were so strong it was making his eyes water.

"She must have lost her mind! Why didn't she clean this mess up." He said to himself.

He wrapped a towel around his nose and went in to open the windows. He grabbed the mop out of the closet and cleaned up his mess with an attitude. When he finished it was about noon so he decided to take a nap. He didn't get much sleep last night with Tonya and all the drinks they had, so sleep was definitely needed at the moment. *"We will talk when she gets home.* He thinks as he lays down and closes his eyes.

He woke up 8 hours later wide awoke. He looked at the clock and thought, *Man I didn't know I was that tired. She didn't even wake me for dinner. It's cool I know she must have put it in the microwave if she had church business. I am starving too.* He walked down the hall and it didn't feel right. The house was pitch black. Sabrina always leaves at least the kitchen light on. I don't smell any food. Once he got to the kitchen the lights were off. The only dishes dirty in the sink were from what he made this morning. Looking in the microwave, the oven and the refrigerator for his plate. He slammed the door shut. *Where is she with my food* he thinks. Okay fine. I'll go to McDonald's and ride by the church she must have some kind of meeting or event.

After he makes it to McDonald's he rides by the church and no one is there. It is completely dark. It doesn't look like anyone has been there either. *Yeah she has lost her mind. I can let the breakfast slide but it is after 9 o'clock. If she is not home when I get back we are going to have big problems.* He thinks to himself as he rushed to get home. What would taken him a 30 minute drive now only took 15 minutes. He pulled up in the driveway and her car was not there.

He goes in the house sits at the kitchen table and eats his food. "I'll give her until 10 I am sure she will have a good reason not to be here with my food." He starts to talk to himself now trying to calm down.
10:15 and no Sabrina and no phone call. He picks up his phone and dials her number. It rings.
She better pick up this phone if she knows what is good for her. No answer! He calls right back. She knows it's important and to pick up if he calls back to back like that. No answer again. He calls two more times and the fifth time she actually declined the call. He looked at the phone like it was a foreign object. *I know she did not just reject my call. So you see me calling you and you're ignoring me. Okay!* He calls again and she rejects the call again but this time he leaves a message. "Sabrina, I don't know what kind of games you're playing but you better be home within an hour. If I have to come find you it will be worse for you. Trust me. Get home now. Have you lost your mind?" He says yelling into the phone.

He is confident that she will be home any minute now so he goes in his man cave, rolls a blunt, gets a beer, smokes, drinks and waits. He falls asleep due to the drugs and alcohol and looks at the time. It's 1:30 in the morning. *She must have snuck in her room so she wouldn't wake me. Oh no, you about to get up and explain yourself. She better pray she has a good reason. It doesn't matter if she does I am still about to beat the brakes off her. She didn't even call to check in.* He says as he walks into their room looking at the bed but Sabrina was not there. He laughs to himself. Looking for her in every room then outside. No car!

"Yup she just signed her death wish." He says out loud he called again and it goes straight to voicemail. Did she block my calls now? He asks himself. Okay think Max What is going on? He starts to think back.

"Sherry, that trick told her she seen Tonya and me together and got her to not come home. It's okay. I know where to find y'all. I'll see you in a few hours ladies." He goes back into the bedroom and goes back to sleep with a smile on his face for what's to happen in the morning.

Chapter 17
The truth will set you free!

Pastor

Pastor was in his office working on his sermon for Sunday. He has not stayed in his home since he left Monday night. The only one that knew he was sleeping at the church was Brother Zachariah and his mother. After Tuesday service he confessed to his mother what all has happened with Tonya. She said he could come home with her instead of sleeping at the church. He declined and said he had everything he needed in these four walls. So she brings him dinner and prays with him. He did stop by his home to get more clothing as well. Tonya was not there which was good because he couldn't bare to look at her at this moment. He could afford a hotel room but he didn't want to risk someone seeing him and he needed to stay as close to God as possible. It was Thursday now so he has gotten used to sleeping on the pull out sofa bed. At around 11 am he heard a knock on his door.

"Come in" He says.

"Hi, Pastor are you busy, I know you told me to bring this to you as soon as I got all the information on Tonya." Zach says with a cream folder in his hand.

"Oh come in Brother. That was fast. Your guy must really take his job seriously." Pastor replied

"Well, let's just say he takes care of his people in a timely fashion." Zachariah smiled talking about God.

"Okay I have no problem with that, what do you have for me?" Pastor says.

"Well take a look for yourself. Remember what I said. Stay focused on God and things will work out." Zach warns handing Pastor the folder with all the information that could either break him or make him stronger.

"Would you like for me to stay with you as you read through it." Zach offered.

"No thanks, something tells me I should be alone for this. I appreciate it and for all your help." Pastor say as he holds the folder with shaking hands.

"Okay remember you have my number and I'll be in my office if you need anything.

"Thanks brother," Pastor says sitting in his chair.

Zachariah walked out of the door and steps to the left of the door. He looked down the hall to make sure no one was looking or coming. He closed his eyes and made himself invisible and walked back through the wall to watch. Pastor was just opening the first page of the background check. The picture was his wife but the name was Shanika Sullivan. The first page shows how she was put in foster care at the age of 12 because her mother murdered her abusive father. At 17, she was arrested for stealing from the mall. That same year arrested for assault and battery and disrupting the peace. At 20 she was arrested for drug possession in an attempt to sell. At 22, she was arrested and did seven years of a ten year sentence in prison for murder that she claims was self defense. At 31 is when she changed her name to Tonya Nicholson later to become Tonya Stevens. No police record for a Tonya Stevens or Nicholson. As he kept going through the photos he came to the photos of her in her car, then in a restaurant receiving a gift. from the man. Only seeing a side view at first then a clear photo of him. It was Max, Sabrina's husband. That's when his heart stopped. Rage filled him. He kept flipping through the pictures of them walking into the hotel and then the photo of them shutting the blinds with Max kissing Tonya's neck.

He slammed the folder shut and stood up and started to pace the floor back and forth. His mind was racing back and forth. *My wife is a killer and a scam artist, she was having an affair with one of his old friends from church and on top of that they have been doing this under my nose for who knows how long. I had no clue that it would be someone that used to be so close to me. I helped him get on his feet and get a job.*

Zachariah stood in the corner unseen and watched as the evil spirits surrounded Pastor. Jealousy, hate, betrayal, unforgiveness, revenge, murder. All of these things floated in and out of Pastor. When Pastor reached for his keys and headed for the door. God told Zachariah.

"GO TO HIM NOW! MAKE HIM REMEMBER ME AND WHO HE IS" God said with urgency.

"Yes Lord, I will" Zach says to God.

As soon as Pastor opened the door Zach was right in front of him. "Hey, I was just coming to see if you needed anything. I am about to go have a early lunch. Want to come? I am not familiar with the area. Can you take me someplace good? I want some soul food like mama used to make." Zach shot off questions trying to keep Pastor from passing him. Zach was a lot taller and muscular than Pastor so it wasn't hard to do.

Pastor took a deep breath looked up to God and said, "Thank you God. Sure I can take you someplace amazing for soul food. It's a little family owned restaurant called Bosco's Baby's Restaurant and Catering. They have the best smothered pork chops. Do you eat pork chops?" Pastor asked.

"Well we will have to see about that. Nobody can cook better than moms." Zach says as they walk outside and get in Pastor's car.

"Do you mind if I turn on the radio? I heard there is a great gospel station here." Zach say.

"Sure it's already programmed in just hit the eject button Rejoice 96.9 I never change the station" Pastor replied smiling.

As they rode, Zach took over the airways and made sure to play songs that would minister to his soul like William Murphy, You are my strength. Trust in you by Anthony Brown and Group Therapy and Todd Dulaney Pulling Me Through. By the time they made it to the restaurant. The evil spirits were gone and Pastor had totally surrendered back to God.

When they sat down to eat Pastor looked at Zach and said "Thank you, I was about to do something stupid. You saved my life and someone else's. How did you know to come back?"

"Well, truth is I never left. You just think I did. I am human and I know the feeling of wanting revenge. I read the file before I gave it to you. I hope you didn't mind. I knew you would need some friendly advice. Or just a distraction if nothing else." Zach replied.

"So, if you were me, what would you do? You read the file you see what she has done and who she is. Do you know the man is Sabrina's husband. This is going to hurt her so bad. How do I get out of this marriage without a fight or humiliation? Clearly she is crazy!" Pastor say rubbing his head.

"Well Pastor I am not you so I can't say what to do. I will say pray about it. God is on your side and what looks like bad God can turn it around and make it good. He is amazing just trust in him." Zach replied in all honesty.

"Yeah, You are right. Do I say anything to Sabrina she should know about this you know?" Pastor says sad for her.

Zach looked up like he was thinking but he was really talking with God. SHE WILL COME TO HIM. God says in Zach's mind.

"Yes, I would tell her if I were you the next time you see her." Zach says.

"Okay I will show her everything. She needs to know what kind of a nutcase my wife is. I would hate for her to be in danger." Pastor states with worry.

"So what do I do about Tonya? Do I go home? I really don't need to see her today.' Pastor replied with all seriousness.

"I would go home but only when you feel you can control yourself. I wouldn't say anything about what you found out today either. The spirit of a person will always come out and expose themselves. Of course you can't pretend that everything is great, try to be as nice and respectful as possible if she wants to talk. If you see she is going to upset you, leave immediately. I would also keep a close eye on her. Being that she knows that you know she is cheating I am pretty sure she might have a getaway plan in the works. One that won't leave her empty handed. She might not even talk to you. You haven't been there pretty much all week." Zach say.

"Okay but not tonight, I'll go tomorrow night. I need to pray and be alone with God for a while before I step one foot in her presence." Pastor says.

"Completely understandable" Zachariah replied.

Chapter 18
The wolf's in Sheep's Clothing

Sabrina

It's Friday morning and Sabrina just made breakfast for her and Sherry. Sherry had already informed her manager what was going on and had alerted the security team not to let him in the building even though she was not there. Once he arrived the manager was going to call and let them know. This would give them the opening for traveling to the church without being seen by him. Because he will not be able to see her he will most likely wait for her until she got off. She knew that Max was very upset from the voicemail on her phone last night and the back to back phone calls. God knows what he has in store for me if he was to catch me. I thank God that Zack gave me the oil and I never leave home without it. It is definitely protecting me from him. I have never left Max before so he probably thinks this is just to upset him. He probably thinks something has happened to me. No, he is a smart man so I am sure he has put two and two together from when Sherry left the restaurant. I am surprised he took this long to try and find me. Sabrina was trying not to worry so much about running into Max but it is hard when you are scared of someone. They are overloaded with cases on restraining orders so he probably won't get served until Monday morning. This gives him open range to try to attack me. I know God has my back along with Sherry but what if.......

Sabrina finished the dishes and went to the prayer closet. She looked in the drawer below the candles and pulled out the Bible. She remembered the word God gave her Tuesday night about fear and read 2 Timothy 1:7 *For God Hath not given us the spirit of fear; but of power, and of love, and of sound mind. Joshua 1:9 Have not I commanded thee? Be strong and of a good courage: be not afraid, neither be thou dismayed: for the Lord thy God is with thee whithersoever thou goest.*

"Lord thank you for your covering. I know this is the beginning of my fight. I will not be discouraged nor afraid for I know that you are with me. I will always look to you for my help and my strength. I know you will not leave me Lord and I thank you and praise your name. In Jesus name Amen.

Sabrina stayed in that room for another hour just praising God and praying. Once she was done she was ready for war. She got dressed and as soon as she tightened up her shoes she heard a knock on her door.

"Come in" Sabrina says.

"Hey just got the call, he is there now looking for you. They won't let him in the building. But they have eyes on him. So if he leaves they will let us know. You ready to go?" Sherry informs Sabrina

"Yes, let's do this. He has called me five times this morning. I am sure I will get more notifications and messages soon." Sabrina says.

"Whatever he says in those messages save them. We can use them in court." Sherry says.

"Okay let's take your car. He will know mine if he rides by the church." Sabrina says.

"He knows my car too so I have a special car for this." Sherry says with a big grin on her face.

The ladies walk into the garage and parked next to their cars is an all black 2018 Audi with four doors and tinted windows. You can look out but no one can see inside. It also changes colors from black to purple at the click of a switch.

"Nice, you really went all 007 on this whole protection thing didn't you." Sabrina asked Sherry smiling as she showed her the change of colors.

"Hey, after what happened with my friend I was determined to do everything I could think of to keep women safe. It just so happens that God blessed me with the funds to do so. Come on get in" Sherry says.

On the way to the church Sherry got a call saying that it looks like he is waiting until she gets off. He even brought flowers and chocolate. Once they pulled up into the parking lot of the church. Sherry parked in the far corner and close to the church. Just riding by you can't see who is parked here because of the trees blocking the view from the street.

They went into the church using Sabrina's key and as they made it to the top of the steps they saw Brother Zachariah coming down the hall just leaving his office.

"Hey ladies, How is it going? It's nice to see you to together." Zach says as he reaches the ladies to give them both hugs.

"Hi, everything is as God wants it at the moment. Is Pastor in I really need to speak with him." Sabrina replied.

"Oh yes, he just got back from lunch, I was on my way to his office to find out who is the CEO of A.C.E. Legaci Foundation." Zach says to the girls.

"Oh really, You don't have to ask Pastor I am right in front of you. Is there something I can help you with?" Sherry asked confused that he would be asking about it.

"Oh Praise God. I wanted to know when was the last donation from the church and how much it was. Also on average what's the normal amount each month?" Zach asked with a concerned look.

"Well we usually get about 500 to 700 a month. Small amounts every week. I haven't actually looked at it this month to see. Being that we haven't had an accountant in about three weeks here at the church. I figured we would get the donation once everything was in order. Is there something wrong?" Sherry replied worried.

"Yes, there is, you should have been getting a lot more than that, come with me. Sabrina do you mind if I borrow Sherry while you talk with Pastor." Zach asked.

"Oh, no, not at all that seems important." Sabrina says as she walks away from them headed to Pastor's office.

She knocks on the door and Pastor opens seconds later. "Oh, Hi, I am sorry if I interrupted you but I need to talk with you. It is very important." Sabrina says. For some reason Pastor just stared at her for a few seconds too long.

"Oh, no, I am sorry, You just look different. Come on in. I was hoping to see you soon. I wanted to talk with you about something as well. Have a seat would you like some water or juice? I have grape, cranberry and apple." Pastor offered.

"Sure, I would like grape it's my favorite. Can I say my peace before you say what you have to say. This is a little weird for me." Sabrina says waiting for her nerves to calm down.

"Sure, go ahead" Pastor reassures her.

"Well, I am leaving my husband Max, well I have left my husband. He has been abusive, controlling and just plain evil towards me for the past two years and I can't take it anymore. I have been praying to God for help and for him not to be upset about me leaving my husband. I know God does not like divorce but I truly feel that he will be okay with this decision. On top of that I know he is cheating on me while I am at church. Just this past week there were fresh scratches on his back and a fresh hickey on his neck. I don't have proof but I think he may be cheating with your wife. Sherry saw them together Wednesday at a restaurant and he gave her my shoes that I had on Tuesday night. They were a gift from Sherry a while back but I could not wear them. He did not let me wear anything that he considered sexy outside of the house, that included shoes. Sherry says when she asked about them Tonya said that I gifted them to her because they were not my style. Since I was at work and you were busy I asked Max to take them to her. I know this may sound crazy but I thought you should at least know. If nothing else for you to be aware that I want nothing to do with my husband and that I am in hiding from him. He is looking for me so he might come here. When and if he comes, he will be very upset so I want you to be ok and prepared." Sherry says out of breath.

"I truly apologize for you having to go through the abuse and I will do anything in my power to make sure you stay safe. You are a blessing to so many and you don't deserve that kind of treatment. As far as my wife goes well, I actually have the proof that you are referring to the cheating. I got this information yesterday." He says handing her the folder on his desk.

Sabrina reached for it looking confused. Once she opened it she gasped for air and put her hand over her mouth. "Oh, my Goodness. Lord who is this child?" Sabrina asked looking up at Pastor.

"Keep reading, That's my wife as a child. Her real name is Shanika Sullivan. I did a background check on her after she confessed to cheating and threatened me if I tried to divorce her. As you can see in the file she will do anything for money which is why she is staying with me, so she says. I wanted to show you this information to warn you that my wife, well soon to be ex wife is crazy and a murderer. I need you to be careful Sabrina." Pastor says just as she got to the photos of Max and Sherry and Tonya at the restaurant. Sherry standing at there table. Then them entering the hotel and the last photo of Max kissing Tonya's neck while she closed the curtain.

Sabrina didn't even know she was crying until Pastor handed her the tissue.

"This is Sherry in the picture I remember that's what she had on when she told me she saw them a few hours prior." Sabrina says flipping back to the picture.

"I didn't know who she was in the photo I didn't really pay attention. Did you come here alone? I want to ask her a couple of things." Pastor says.

"No she is with Zachariah. They were talking about an account for the God's Helping Hands Shelter. Something is not right with the donations or something." Sabrina replied.

"Ok, can you hold on for one minute Sabrina? I need to make a call." Pastor asked.

"Sure!" Sabrina says.

Pastor went back around his desk and hit the button on his Phone

"Brother Zach, Is Sherry still with you? I need to see her and you as well. I would like to see what you are looking at." Pastor asked.

"No problem sir, we will be there in just a minute" Zach replied.

"This is crazy, Her real name is not Tonya?" Sabrina asked.

"No, she changed her name when she moved here. She was born and raised in California. I have to say, on Tuesday night when you gave that word from God you really helped me out in more ways than one. I was too busy with God's work and wanting someone that shared the same love for God that I didn't even ask God if she was of Him? Did He even know her? I just assumed that because she was here with me, helping me do His will, she had to be sent from God. I was blinded by the flesh. I am sorry that you and your husband have to be apart of my mess. I would have felt a little better if I didn't know you guys personally. You know what I mean?" Pastor confessed.

"Yeah, I know what you mean. I understand as well, I am in the same boat." Sabrina replied.

Although I am a little nervous about what may happen if he finds me, I hold on to faith that God has me covered. He won't let me die. I know that for a fact." Sabrina says with confidence.

"I just can't imagine what kind of man would abuse a woman, let alone a woman of God. He should know nothing good will come from it. He was a fool to mistreat you the way he has." Pastor Says.

"Thank you Pastor" Sabrina says.

For the first time Pastor actually looked at Sabrina. Yes she was beautiful but it was like he was now seeing her as a whole new woman of God. Her face has this glow to it. Like she is truly happy and at peace. Her curly hair was hanging around her face instead of in a ponytail. She wore only eyeliner and lipstick and makeup. She had on a t-shirt with the v-neckline and fitting jeans that were not tight but you could still notice her shape. *Yeah he was a fool.* Pastor thought to himself.

There was a knock at the door and Sherry and Zachariah came in. Zach was holding his laptop in his hand.

"Sherry will you look at this. Pastor is it okay if she sees the files?" Sabrina asked Pastor.

"Sure, it's fine I trust Sherry will keep this information to herself. I will inform my mother later on today. The people in this room and mother are the only ones that need to know about this file. Until God tells me what to do next." Pastor stated.

Sabrina handed Sherry the folder and as she scanned through it her facial expression went from shocked, to sad, to horrified and angry all in a matter of two minutes once she reached the end.

"So you knew about them Pastor before Sabrina came in here to tell you?" Sherry asked confused.

"Well, I just got this information yesterday but she confessed to cheating on Monday night. I have been staying here at the office ever since. I needed to figure out what to do." Pastor says to them.

"I am sorry Pastor but I think there is more, Zach can you show him." Sherry says to Pastor.

"Well after looking at the accounts and calling the banks. Sherry here verified that the donation amount was off. Someone was taking $4,000 from the church account but is only putting like $600 to $700 dollars into the shelter each month. It should be the whole $4,000 or close to whatever was donated. Each month they get around the same amount. The last withdraw was the beginning of this month. Three weeks ago. It's just not adding up." Zachariah explained to them.

"Three weeks ago? That was right when Tamika moved away. She might know something about this. She handled the accounts for the shelter and the church." Sherry said angrily.

Pastor had to sit down. This was too much for him to handle. He knew that Tonya was only with him for the money now, but he would have never thought she would steal from the church too. He felt like he provided her with everything she needed and more. Why would she do this?

"Well where is the money going to?" Sabrina asked.

"Give me one minute, that is pulling up now." Zach says responding to her question.

"Lord, how have they been paying the bills and getting supplies they need? That is nowhere near enough to take care of all the things needed. That barely helps with food" Pastor asked.

"Well, I am the CEO, I have given a lot of money and other organizations donate as well. By God's grace we are still open. I would give my last to keep that place open if I had too" Sherry says with confidence.

"Okay, this say that it goes to a Bank of America in Greer, SC. There are two names on the account. Of course I can't see who but I can make a few phone calls and see what I can find out." Zach says.

"Lord, wasn't Tonya and Tamika like best friends at one point. They kind of fell apart about 6 months ago." Sherry says to the group.

"Yeah, but does anyone have contact information for Tamika. She left all of a sudden you know." Sabrina says.

"I can find her, my guy can find anybody. I just need her full name." Zach says referring to God.

"Tamika Wilson was her name. Are there any other financial issues anywhere else in the church Zachariah" Pastor says in a sad voice.

"No Pastor, she was actually a good accountant. Everything else adds up to the last cent everywhere." Zach informs Pastor.

"Good, Zach, please go see if you can find Tamika and see who the names are on the account that the money is being transferred too." Pastor says.

"Yes sir, I am on it." Zach says leaving the office with his computer.

Sherry's phone rings in her pocket.

"Hello, Sherry, He just pulled off. If you are not in your safe place get there now. He was not happy. We almost had to call the police when he tried to sneak in with an employee." Kim, their office manager says in the phone.

"Okay Thank you Kim." Sherry says looking at Sabrina. "Well, that's our cue, we have to go now." Sherry says looking at Sabrina.

"Okay" Sabrina says getting out of the chair.

"Sherry, Sabrina if you need anything don't hesitate to call me. I don't care what time it is ok." Pastor says walking them to the door.

"Thank you Pastor, you be careful. I am pretty sure his next stop will be here looking for me. So stay alert." Sabrina says.

"Oh don't worry about me. I wasn't always a Pastor. I am licensed to carry and if he comes here looking for you he better pray that God stays with me. I am still human and I have to fight these demons too. This is a fight he does not want at this moment." Pastor says with reassurance.

"Okay, Pastor got a lil hood in him, I see you Pastor!" Sherry jokes.

"Okay get going, Sherry, I will keep you posted on the account information and keep Sabrina safe please. She is a valuable asset to the Kingdom of God." Pastor says to Sherry looking at Sabrina.

"I am on it Pastor" Sherry says as they walk out the door.

Once the girls were in the car, no more than ten minutes later, Pastor sees Max's car ride by the church at a very slow pace. He didn't try to come in he was just looking for her car.

Chapter 19

Getting ready to fight

Pastor

Pastor was finally getting ready to go home. With the information he had on file and what Sabrina told her about Max God really had his hands full with these two. It was 9pm Friday night before he left the church. He had to do some last minute praying and filling his head with the word of God. This was not about to be an easy task, but he was determined to pass this test. Once he pulled up into his garage he noticed that Tonya was not home. *Thank you God* he thought in his head. He was ready but not as soon as he got home.

Once he walked in the door immediately a foul odor hit his nostrils. He looked around the house and you didn't have to think the smell was coming from the trash. It was the whole house. It looked like someone had a party and did not clean up for a week. Dishes were in the sink, the floors had sticky juice and beer on them, empty beer and wine bottles everywhere. Old wet towels in the bathroom, clothes everywhere. It was not the home he was used too. *Lord she is truly showing herself now. This is crazy* he thought to himself. He went to put his clothes and bags in his room and turned on his surround sound system to Rejoice 96.9 radio station. *Lord send your angels it's time to clean house.* Pastor says to himself, After he goes into his prayer closet for his anointing oil.

Just then Zachariah appeared beside him in the spiritual realm in his battle clothes. Pastor could not see him or feel him. As Pastor started cleaning in the living room the evil spirits noticed Zachariah and shivered in fear in the corners of the room. Once Pastor was done with the cleaning he prayed over the room, anointed the room and moved on to the next. As soon as Pastor started to pray the spirits got mad and attacked Zachariah in the spirit realm. There was drunkenness, lust, anger, revenge, and betrayal. Just some of the spirits she left there. Zachariah quickly pulled out his sword and started slashing left and right. Once Pastor anointed the room the evil spirits were cast down into the pits of hell. They did this routine twelve times, Pastor didn't leave one room or closet untouched. Nor did Zachariah. By the time they finished it was two o'clock in the morning. Pastor took a shower and went to bed. Tonya was not home but he didn't care, he needed the peace.

The next morning Pastor woke up at like 9 am. He decide he needed to go for a jog to get his mind right. He said his morning prayer, brushed his teeth, put on his jogging shorts and a t-shirt and walked out the door. Before he could make it to the end of the block he saw Tonya pulling into the driveway. He ran for about an hour and a half. Sometimes walking while he listened to the audio Bible in his Bluetooth headphones. Once he made it home she was just getting out of the shower. He gathered his clothes so he could go in after her and when she came out they both looked at each other.

"Good Morning Tonya" Pastor says to her.

"Good morning" she replied not knowing what else to say. So they both went their separate ways.

Once Pastor got dressed he went to the kitchen to make breakfast. It was really quiet so he went to see what Tonya was doing. He found her in his office typing something. He couldn't see much because the door was half closed. He walked further away from the door.

"Tonya, are you hungry? Have you eaten breakfast yet?" He asked hoping that would get her off his computer.

"No, I haven't eaten" She says back knowing that he seen her on the computer.

"Okay, I am making a cheese omelet and toast with turkey bacon, Would you like some?" He asked being as nice as he could.

"Sure, that would be great. Thank you. I will be there in a minute. Just working on something." She says trying to finish up the last of it her letter and print it.

"Okay, take your time" Pastor says.

Thank you God for making this easy. I know she is up to something but I will just play dumb like I am over it all. Pastor thinks.

As they sat down to eat there was silence. Neither one really looking at the other.

"Tonya, I just have to tell you that I forgive you for cheating and whatever else you have done. I know you didn't ask for my forgiveness but I have to forgive you. I do love you and I pray nothing but the best for you. I apologize for leaving the way I did. I had to clear my mind and figure out what to do next. I understand if you don't want to talk about it and I am completely okay with that. I just had to get that off my chest." Pastor says in all honesty.

"Well thank you. You have no idea how that makes me feel. I forgive you for leaving as well. I have to say it was actually a good thing though. I think we both needed some time away. I would not like to bring this up ever again. I am going to be better. I will be in church with you this Sunday. Thank you baby" Sabrina say getting up to give him a hug and a kiss on the cheek. That kiss made Pastor think of Jesus and Judas in the Garden. *Lord she is about to betray us as Judas did!* Pastor thought to himself.

He didn't say anything he just went back to eating his food. Pastor went to his prayer room and prepared the rest of his sermon for tomorrow.

They didn't say much to each other the rest of the day. She was in one room doing something and he in the other.

Chapter 20

Anger and confusion

Max

Max was furious Saturday morning when he went to Sabrina's job and they would not let him in. He went by the church and she was not there either. Clearly she is hiding and doesn't want to be found. *She's about to leave me he thought but where the hell is she. I went by her job, the shelter, Sherry's house and even the church. She doesn't hang with anyone but Sherry and me. I know she knows where she is because she is missing as well.* Max remembered the way Sherry looked at him at the restaurant. *I know she went and told Sabrina what she saw, plus the way I have been treating Sabrina was just the fuel to the fire for her to leave me. I have to get her back!* He thought to himself.

If I stop being lazy I could always find a job but I can't afford this house without her. She could do it on her own but not with my construction jobs only lasting months at a time. I haven't actually went to work in a little over a year. So finding work might be a little harder with that big gap on my resume.

He picked up the phone to call Tonya

"Hey man, have you seen Sabrina, Sherry, or your husband. Sabrina has been gone for 2 days and I can't find her anywhere!" Max says as soon as she picks up the phone

"That is perfect timing" Tonya says excited.

"What the hell do you mean that is perfect! My wife left me and you're talking about that's perfect!" Max replies angrily.

"Man calm down and listen! Remember the plan, you're supposed to go to the church tomorrow to cause a distraction and accuse the accountant of sleeping with her. Now that she is missing you can accuse him of stealing her from you. I'm going to slip in Pastor's office and leave the letter. The accountant will be fired so we can later get access to the account and transfer the money into our account. My husband has finally decided to come home so I have to try and get on his good side even though the sight of him makes me sick. So don't screw this up for me! Wait until tomorrow and I'll have everything worked out, okay?" She says irritated that he was not cooperating.

"Okay now, you better not play me Tonya!" Max says serious and angry at everybody including himself for getting involved with her.

"Whatever, you need me. If I wanted to play you I could have done it a long time ago. You are nowhere near man enough for me to even have to try and play you. You do and believe everything I say. You are weak so you prey on people that won't defend themselves. Let's be clear! The only reason I keep you around is for sex and to have fun when I can get away from all this church and God mess. Don't ever think that I need you or that I am scared of you. This isn't love or anything else, this is just business!" Tonya snaps on him.

"Alright Tonya, you try and play me if you want to and I will kill you! This is my life we are talking about!" states Max angrily.

"Ha! I am not about to repeat myself. You can try it! I have my part of the plan to do. Now if you will excuse me I have to sweet talk my husband. You just make sure you are there at 12:30 after church service!" Tonya says with an attitude before she went into the house Saturday morning.

Max stared at his phone angry and confused. *What am I going to do? Alright, I'll be there to get my wife back for sure. If I have to make a deal with this crazy psycho I will. If it just so happens to help me get some extra money then I'll act a fool! No problem! I need some answers and somebody is going to give them to me!* Max thought to himself. The rest of the day he just got drunk and high and waited for Sunday morning to come.

Chapter 21
The fight of your life

Sabrina

Saturday was easy for Sabrina. Sherry and Sabrina worked on her self defense moves all day. They took a break to relax by the pool and after dinner they started another session of training before bedtime. They were not going to let the enemy stop them from attending church this Sunday morning or praising God. They decided to sit up in the balcony and get there early so no one would see them. The church was huge so there was plenty of room for them only a few people would sit up here so the seats were all empty. Which also gave them a great escape route if they needed it. Today will tell Sabrina a lot about how her life will be in the few days to come. Will this be an easy divorce or drama filled? Will she be happy and safe or afraid and hiding constantly. She knows her husband, and he knows her so he will come to the church looking for her. She was ready! Sherry has already informed the members of church security of Max and for them to keep an eye on him. They technically have to let him in because it is a public place but if he starts any trouble they are to stop him and escort him off the premises.

Before the ladies arrived at church Mother Mary, Sherry, and Sabrina did a conference prayer call this morning. Mother Mary knew that today would be a very hard day. War was coming to them in the spiritual form and natural form. God had His work cut out for him as well as his angels, but Mother Mary was confident in her God and so was Sabrina and Sherry.

As service got started praise and worship did their one selection and there was prayer, two more songs from the praise and worship, tithes and offerings were taken up and then Pastor Jonathan got up to do his sermon.

"Today we are going to read from two chapters in the Bible Mark 11:26 says *but if you do not forgive neither will your father in Heaven forgive your transgressions and Matthew 6:14 for if you forgive others their trespasses the recklessness willful sins your heavenly father will also forgive you*. How many of you have ever been betrayed, lied on, cheated on, abused, and just all-around mistreated in life. Well this week has been very trying for me as well. I have gone through a number of emotions and I feel that I must speak on the word forgiveness. The Bible says that if you don't forgive those that trespass against you then the Father in heaven will not forgive you. I don't know about you but that is something that does not sit well with my spirit. I need God in my life more than anybody can ever imagine. So I can not let what somebody else did to me because of their own personal reasons, setbacks in life or past relationships make me go to hell. Life is hard and comes with many troubles but God has a plan for each one of us. If you follow and obey him he will turn your bad into good. I can tell you that it will not be easy and it will not happen overnight but you have to be willing to fast, pray, and speak with God on a daily basis. Some days more than once or twice a day. If you don't do these things then you will forever be trapped and they will always have the power over you. If you don't know if you have forgiven someone that has done you wrong here is your answer. If you can sit in the same room with that person and not feel any type of animosity or hate feelings toward that person you're over it. If you try to talk about the situation that may have happened and you cry and get upset. You are not over it and that is when you need to go to God and ask for help, deliverance and guidance. No, I'm not saying that after you forgive someone that you have to continuously be in their presence and be around them because you never forget what happened. God gave us wisdom and to not be fools. What you can do is you can continuously pray for them. Check on them every blue moon and if God says so bless them with whatever God says for you to bless them with. You never know what's really going on inside of someone else's brain! You never know what's really going on inside of someone else's home! You never know what has happened in their childhood or what happened yesterday. So don't be so quick to sin in anger because of what someone else has done to you. This will lead to a road of destruction, not just for yourself but for the other person as well. If you feel like someone has done you wrong go to that person in private and if that person won't listen, take a mutual friend with you to speak with that person if they still won't listen continue to pray for them. Everyone does not want to be the bigger person and everyone will not want to change. Just make sure you do your part to get you into the pearly gates. Even while Jesus was being crucified he still forgave them. While he had nails in his feet and hands. That is the power of God and what we have inside of us. Forgiveness is not easy but it is necessary. God has a greater plan for our hard times and he will sometimes use it to show you how great he is and how he can use it to bless you. Most life trials are for your testimony and to show people that God will always come out victorious!" Pastor say. The church had a quiet sniffling sound in the air. Everyone was struggling with something that they either needed forgiveness from or had to forgive someone.

Sabrina was in the balcony crying right alongside Sherry. The girls stayed in their seats while service was being dismissed. Sabrina looked to her right and she didn't notice at first but Tonya was seated in the front row on the opposite side of Mother Mary and Zachariah. She looked down at the woman and began to pray. Then she looked at Sherry who had just noticed her as well.

"Well, if she is here I am sure Max is here as well. We will stay seated and see what happens." Sherry says.

Not even 5 seconds later.

"Where is this accountant called Zeck or Zach!" Max yells at the top of his lungs. "You have my wife and you have been sleeping with her. I want her back now or it's going to be really bad for you brother." Max says as he walks up on Zach.

Shocked from the outburst everyone turned to look at Max and Zach. For some reason security should have jumped in by now but they were nowhere in the sanctuary. God had distracted all security with something else to do. This was something that no man could stop. Sabrina was frozen and in shock from the accusations. What in the world would make him think she was sleeping with Zach of all people Sabrina thought. Just like that Tonya was not in the room anymore.

"Where did she go" Sabrina asked Sherry.

"What? Who?" Sherry says not taking her eyes off the two men. She had to protect Sabrina and her only threat was down there acting a fool.

"Tonya, she was in here but now she is gone." Sabrina says.

"I don't know and I don't care but we need to get you out of here" Sherry says pulling on Sabrina's arm for her to follow her.

Max was in front of Zach now. He suddenly got hot just standing in front of him. They don't make eye contact.

"Where is my wife punk?" Max says looking at Zach's chest. Frustrated that he was sweating bullets and he has not gotten an answer Max swings at Zach but Zach catches his arm with the back of his forearm. Max swings with his free hand and Zach catches that one too. Max is forced to look into Zachariah's eyes because he could not break hold of the grip that Zach had on him. Instantly Max feels like he is on fire. Max starts to scream but nothing comes out. Max starts to have a heart attack and falls to the floor.

The girls hurry down the back steps of the balcony and towards the back door. They stop in their tracks as they hear a gunshot come from behind them. Then two shots hit the glass window and breaks.

"Jesus!" Sabrina cries. *Lord whatever happens please don't let me die. I know he is going to shoot me.* She say to herself as she turns around.

Pure shock struck both their faces when they turn to see Tonya pointing a gun at them and not Max. She was so close that the gun was in arm's length. Sherry grabbed Sabrina's hand in reassurance that it would be ok.

"Tonya, what are you doing" Sabrina asked confused and scared. She remembers the file she read on this woman. She used the oil but she wasn't sure it would help her with Tonya.

"Oh just taking what's rightfully mine. You see, this is the offering money and it is more than enough for me to move far away from here and get another identity. I have been here far too long. I should have listened to Tamika before I married that sorry piece of man. He is so weak, too caring, and too nice. That type of stuff makes him a easy target. Just like you" She says still holding the gun. The girls didn't notice the backpack in her hand until she mentioned it.

"What does Tamika have to do with this?" Sherry asked just to keep her talking and stalling until someone could get over here to them. They probably didn't even hear the shots with all the screaming going on upstairs. *Lord what is going on up there?*

"Oh, she helped me put all this together, until she got a conscience and left me here. She wouldn't even give me access to setup the account transfers myself. It's ok. I came up with a better quicker plan. Now if you will excuse me I have to go. Move. Oh and thank you for the shoes Sabrina they fit great. I enjoyed having them on while I was with your husband too. I am going to miss him…"

Before she could finish her sentence Zach had distracted her long enough by coming down the stairs for Sherry to push the gun away and kick her in the face. The blow was so hard that the gun went off and hit Sabrina. Sherry lost it and continued to kick and beat up Tonya until Pastor came and got her off her. She was a bloody and unconscious mess. Sherry immediately ran to Sabrina's side with Zach holding pressure to the gunshot wound in her chest. She was losing a lot of blood and fast.

The last thing she remembers was Sherry screaming "Call the ambulance now!" It all went black.

Sabrina woke up to a bright light in her face the atmosphere was very calm, the breeze was the fresh smell of flowers and she felt like she was having a massage all over her body. She was standing in her safe place inside of the church sanctuary but it was just her. This was her heaven. She turned and looked around she saw a man walking towards her up the alleys. Behind him was a beautiful blue and white sky full of clouds. He had broad shoulders, long dreaded hair, caramel complexion, and light brown eyes. It was Zachariah.

"Zachariah where am I? What is this place? What are you doing here?" she looked around confused.

"Come take a walk with me Sabrina. I have a lot to tell you in very little time you are currently in heaven. You have died but your work on Earth is not done. God has many gifts and blessings to bestow upon you. This is why you had to go through your trials and tribulations in order to get you ready for your true purpose and blessings. You will speak to nations about what you've been through and lead millions of people to God and His glory. Your new husband has been called for the same fate as you. God will reveal him to you as soon as you wake up and go back to Earth. He will be the first man you see."

"But how are you here and not on Earth with me this doesn't make any sense" Sabrina asked.

"You remember all those times that you prayed to God to send you help to get you out of the situation you were in? Well I am that help. I am one of God's angels Armies of War. I was also sent to help Pastor Johnathan as well. No one knows that I am an angel unless God wants that person to know and we like to keep it that way. God remembered you Sabrina and you will be blessed. Stay close to Sherry. She is your Ruth and you need her just as much as she needs you. It's time for you to wake up." Zachariah replied.

Okay but will you be there when I wake up?" Sabrina asked.

"Yes, I have more work to do. Your part is done. God is pleased with you" Zachariah says fading away and she wakes up in her hospital bed. The beeping and cold air filled her nostrils and she began to cough a little and pain erupted in her chest. *Thank you God I am all yours! Use me as you will!* Sabrina thinks to herself and she feels someone touch her hand.

"Oh, thank you God! You are finally awake. I was so worried about you" Pastor Jonathan says squeezing her hand.
"Pastor!" Sabrina tried to say in shock but her chest hurts.

"Hold on let me call the nurse. You must be in pain?"

Really God! Pastor Jonathan is supposed to be my husband. You really do have a sense of humor! We will talk about this later! Laughing to herself she says to God in her head.

Chapter 22
Let's rebuild

Pastor Jonathan
Two months later
Pastor Jonathan was so relieved when Sabrina finally woke up from a coma she had been out for a whole week. She had stopped breathing on the way to the hospital for ten whole minutes. The congregation had a night of prayer on that Tuesday. Pastor didn't lose faith in God. He knew that she had more work to be done here on earth. The bullet pierced her lung three inches away from her heart which caused her to lose a lot of blood in a fast amount of time. Thank God that the ambulance was already on their way for Max. Sabrina did not know what was going on with Max until Sherry told her a couple days later when she was able to actually talk without hurting herself. She was amazed at how God works. Here she thought she would still have to worry about him but God is taking care of that. It goes to show you don't have to fight your enemy or get revenge on them. Put it in God's hand and he will take care of it for you. She didn't have to press charges on him God has given him his punishment. God is in the process of reconstructing his heart. The things of his past have left his heart hard and full of anger, hate and distrust. He will never be the same again when God gets done with him. Their divorce will be final in a couple of months.

I've had to do press conferences, phone calls, and meeting after meetings. Surprisingly, the congregation has grown to over five hundred members. All wanting to give, help and donate to A.C.E. Legaci Foundation and to help pay for Sabrina's medical bills. She hasn't had to pay one dime. God is amazing, he has this way of taking your troubles and turning them around for your good. Sabrina has a full schedule of T.V. shows, radio station interviews, magazines interviews and she was offered to turn her story into a book and later a movie. She is a walking miracle and the world needs to know what God has done for her.

 Everyone is trying to figure out what's going on in my church? How did she survive? Did Max die? Do you still have faith in God? I've had these questions asked over and over and over again. I give the same response every time. "As you can see Sabrina is not dead, she is a miracle and you will see her do wonderful things. My faith in God has grown stronger over the past months with all the trials and tribulations we've been through as a church family. Many blessing have come as well." Pastor would always reply with faith in his heart.

Zachariah was placed in jail for 3 days due to conspiracy of stealing money from the church. A letter they found in my office implying that he was a pimp and that Tamika, our old accountant left and ran away from him. So he came to replace her to keep the money flowing in. Tamika actually called Pastor Jonathan on behalf of Zachariah. She saw everything that happened at the church on the news and wanted to clear her name. This was her chance to officially apologize to Pastor for the help that she did provide Tonya before she left. She explained to him the reason she left was because she was convicted by God and he told her that if she stayed she would die early in age and no blessings would ever come to her. Tamika also is going to testify against Tonya providing the fact that she wasn't brought up on any charges herself. She has changed her life around and wants to stay in that place where God is pleased with her. Tonya is being held in jail and is due to go to court within a month for attempted murder and robbery. She claims that Zachariah has visited her in her cell. That he set her on fire for three nights in a row when she first went to jail. She is being evaluated for Schizophrenia. My divorce will be final in a few months as well. Sabrina and I actually went and filed for divorce together. Crazy right?

Zachariah is still the accountant at Church of Christ. The congregation of course was a little hard on him until the police proved that Tonya wrote that letter from my office the day before the shooting. Thank God for Google Docs, it saves everything and it is easy to find what you thought was deleted. They did a full investigation on her and found out that she was wanted for murder in California as well. She killed a big time drug dealer in an attempt to rob him in his house after a date. This is why she came to South Carolina. She won't be getting out of prison anytime soon.

Sherry has been by Sabrina's side everyday. She has been her maid, her stylist, her driver, her everything. When she is in a good mood I can convince her to let me take Sabrina out on a date. Nothing big, just dating. We are Kingdom people and we live by Kingdom rules. This is all God's plan and we are keeping our eyes on him first and for what to do next.

Chapter 23
The beginning of a new life

Mother Mary
2 Years later

Mother Mary woke up excited this Saturday morning. *This is the day that the Lord has made and I rejoice and be glad in it!* She sings in her head as she gets ready for the day. Today Pastor Sabrina Smith and Apostle Jonathan Stevens my son are finally getting married! They dated for a year and then were engaged for another year. This has been the longest two year wait of my life. I kept asking them what they were waiting for? They know that they were brought together by God. They said that they are following orders. Doing things the right way as God has instructed them to do. They had already vowed to never rush into another relationship again. So after being instructed by God to wait two years that is what they did. It was hard sometimes for them and I would laugh at them because their hormones were all out of control sometimes. I couldn't really argue with God's instructions but I am well over to the age of needing some grandbabies so they need to come on with it. So now after the long wait they can start working on my little prophets and miracle workers. Yes! It's a blessed day!

This wedding is the biggest wedding I have ever seen. There is only one bridesmaid and one best man but the number of people that will be in attendance is crazy. They are having a private ceremony with just family and church members only. The rest of the world is welcome to the reception. It is estimated to be over one thousand people in attendance. After the shooting at the church, the congregation tripled in attendance and every Sunday now the seats are full. With the anointing that is on Sabrina and Jonathan now they have reached millions of people all over the world speaking at different churches all over the world. I find myself getting tired just watching them. They always make sure they are home for Sunday and Tuesday service at Church of Christ my late husband Joseph's church. What you thought I didn't have a husband? He passed it down to our son Jonathan a year before he died in his sleep. God said his work was done and that he had raised Jonathan just as God told him to. Sometimes our purpose in the Kingdom is to simply raise God's servants for their time to reign. My job is to help keep them in order and a number of other things. I will be on this Earth a long time, but I look forward to being with my Father and my husband in heaven one day.

A year after the shooting Zachariah left and said God called him to move to another job at a college. I know that he had other Godly business to handle in the Kingdom. God is amazing because Zach came to me in a dream and said he would see me soon last week. So I hope he will show his face for this miracle that he helped put together.

Once Mother was dressed she went to the church to help out in any way she could. The bride and the groom were both a nervous wreck so she had to calm them both down. They haven't seen each other in a week. They keep asking her "Is she here" Is he here Mother?" It was so cute at how in love they were. It's funny how at first they never even looked at each other in that way. Now they are about to be married. Sherry was with Sabrina putting her shoes on her and I was looking for her necklace when a knock came to the door.

"I'll get it!" Mother Mary says.

She opened the door and Zachariah was standing there in an all white three piece suit and black shoes.

"Oh praise God I was hoping you could make it. God is so amazing" Mother Mary says reaching up to give him a hug.

"Hello Mother Mary, it is always a pleasure to see you again." Zach says smiling from ear to ear.

"Heyyyyy Zach, Don't you still look sent from heaven" Sherry laughs and gives him a hug followed by Sabrina.

"Yeah well you know, God keeps using me so he makes me look this good" Zach laughs looking from Sherry to Sabrina. "I just wanted to stop in and say hi. I won't make it to the reception but I couldn't miss the ceremony. Sabrina, you look as beautiful as a angel." Zach says.

"Thank you Zach" Sabrina replies.

Sabrina had on a ivory strapless dress with diamond covering just the top portion of her bust. A diamond belt around the waist that flowed into a tight mermaid style gown. Her hair was curled and flowing around her face with just the right amount of make up for her to look like she didn't have any on with a light pink lipstick. Her shoes were silver open toe high heels to match the dress.

"How is the new accountant Michael doing Sherry. He is not giving you any problems is he? He came highly recommended from the college I work for." Zach asked Sherry.

"Oh, he is great, he knows his stuff, very, smart and respectful. Thank you for recommending him. He is also a big help at the shelter when I am away with Sabrina at her speaking engagements. Now that I think about it. He is like my personal assistant" Sherry says thinking of Michael. He is very handsome now that she thinks about it a little more too.

"Good to hear that, I also wanted to tell you that God has been watching you and he is pleased. Continue what you're doing. He remembers you. Your blessing is on the way." Zach says to Sherry knowing what God has in store for her next. Just as Sabrina was tested she will be too and her husband she has already met.

"Well praise God, tell me, how is it that you always have a word from God" Sherry asked looking at Zach.

Mother Mary and Sabrina looked at each other. They both knew who and what he truly was but Sherry did not. They have talked about it before together.

"SHOW HER" says God to Zachariah

Zach looked at both Sabrina and Mother Mary smiled and winked as he took a step back a couple of feet.

"Well, I am not your ordinary accountant." Zachariah says as he closed his eyes and his whole body began to glow. Light shined from his head and finger tips. Slowly his wings unfolded from behind him through his clothing. They were all white feathers, and were the length of his two arms put together.

"I am very close to the Father and was sent here to Cast Down all your enemies back into the pits of hell. For God remembers you! It is finished." Zach says in a much deeper and demanding voice. Then he just disappeared into thin air.

All three women just stared in amazement at the spot that Zach once was, not able to say a word.

They all looked at each other smiled and gave God so much praise for blessing them in so many ways. Their faith and commitment to God will never wither or fade. They had much work to do. The End

Thank you for reading I truly hope that you enjoyed the book and I pray that it blesses you. I pray this book has changed your heart in some way and you look to God for all that you do in life. If you do not know God as your personal Lord and savior it is never too late to get to know him all you have to do is confess with your mouth and believe in your heart that Jesus died and rose again to deliver us from our sins. I strongly encourage you to get into a faith-based home church where you can be fed the word of God daily. God is amazing and he can truly change your life you just have to be willing to accept him in your heart and commit to his word.

Please be on the lookout for my next book. Sherry is up next and she will have to face her inner demons of low- self esteem, shame, and neglect.

Helpful resources

National Domestic Violence Hotline
1 - 800 - 799 - SAFE (7233)
www.thehotline.Org

National child abuse hotline

1-800-4- a- child (1-800-422-4453)
www.childhelp.org

National Alliance on Mental Illness
1-800-950-Nami (6264)
www.nami.org

National Red Cross
1-800 -Red-Cross (2767)
www.redcross.org

Salvation Army
www.salvationarmyusa.org

National Suicide Hotline
1 800-273- talk 8255
www.SuicidePreventionLifeline.Org

Sexual assault hotline
1-800-223-5001
www.nsvrc.org

AAA Crisis Pregnancy Center
+1-800-560-0717

National Center for PTSD
www.ptsd.va.gov

National Abortion recovery help
866-482-life (5433)
www.Nationalhelpline.Org

About the author

Cherell Evans Latimer is motivational speaker, mother, wife, survivor and a true woman of God. Once a victim of domestic violence including mental, physical, and sexual assault Cherell found hope through her faith in God and is taking her life back. She comes to encourage others to do the same as well. This Greenville resident's lifestyle of love and honor to God is contagious and promotes a sense of peace, humility, and inspiration. Her first book The Wrong Kind of Love- Defined by God started her on this journey. She discusses healthy love, and platforms of understanding how God defines and shapes our lives. She is an incredible asset to the domestic violence survivalist movement and looks forward to working as a resource for others.

www.ingramcontent.com/pod-product-compliance
Lightning Source LLC
Chambersburg PA
CBHW062000040426
42447CB00010B/1842